Hertfordshire
COUNTY COUNCIL
Community Information

AOL 385. 312

‐ 5 JUN 2000

1 3 AUG 2010

9/12

‐ 2 JUL 2001

1 0 DEC 2001

4/5/04

‐ 2 APR 2007

2 0 DEC 2008

Please renew/return this item by the last date shown.

So that your telephone call is charged at local rate,
please call the numbers as set out below:

	From Area codes 01923 or 020:	From the rest of Herts:
Renewals:	01923 471373	01438 737373
Enquiries:	01923 471333	01438 737333
Minicom:	01923 471599	01438 737599

L32

D1470682

EUROTUNNEL

THE ILLUSTRATED JOURNEY

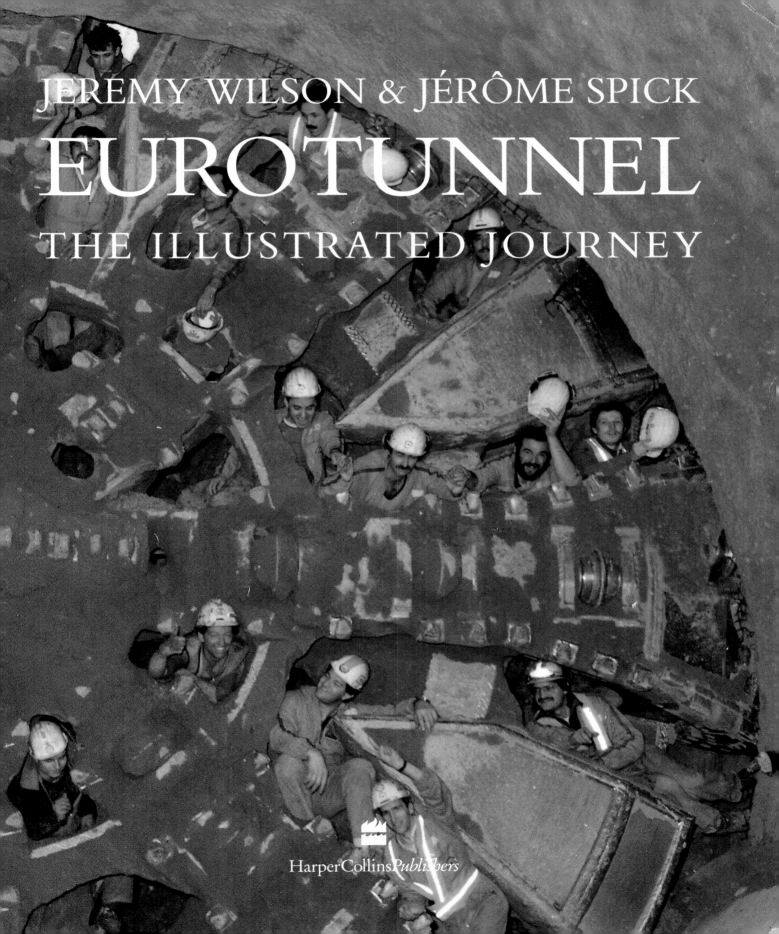

JEREMY WILSON & JÉRÔME SPICK
EUROTUNNEL
THE ILLUSTRATED JOURNEY

HarperCollins*Publishers*

HarperCollins*Publishers*
77-85 Fulham Palace Road,
Hammersmith, London W6 8JB

Published by HarperCollins*Publishers* 1994
1 3 5 7 9 8 6 4 2

A catalogue record for this book is available from the
British Library

ISBN (Special Hardback edition) 1 872009 48 4
ISBN (paperback edition) 0 00 255539 5

Designed by Visible Edge, London
Printed in Great Britain by
Butler & Tanner Ltd, Frome and London

CONTENTS

André Bénard KBE

Co-Chairman, Eurotunnel

The Channel Tunnel, portrayed in this book, has been an exemplary project in many ways.

First, it is the result of the determination, perseverance, courage and imagination of generations of engineers and entrepreneurs. A tunnel was envisaged as early as 1751 and defined as a project in 1802. Work started on both sides of the Channel in 1881 and again in 1974, but was halted on each occasion. At last, between 1986 and 1994, the Channel Tunnel and its transport system have been completed.

Secondly, it has been a model of international co-operation - binational for the construction companies, international for the sources of equipment and technology, and worldwide for the financing. Eurotunnel, the concessionaire, has established its own unique Anglo-French culture.

The project represents both a symbolic step and a real contribution to the future development of Europe. It was the catalyst which launched the high-speed European railway network. By opening the way to new traffic between Britain and the Continent, it is likely to bring enormous economic benefits.

It has provided a model of very complex private financing for a very large infrastructure project. This may help to break down the artificial yet effective frontiers which, in the public mind, set apart or even in opposition the interests of state and private enterprise. The opportunity now exists for a new dynamism in investment and human activity.

Lastly, I think that the Tunnel succeeds in combining aesthetic appeal with efficiency. This great and complex scheme is devoted to a humble purpose, and its huge construction works have been carried out with respect for the environment.

These are the thoughts which I hope will emerge as readers appreciate the many and spectacular facets of this immense project.

27 April 1989. Alastair Morton *(left)* and André Bénard at the French portal after the first breakthrough by a tunnel boring machine.

Sir Alastair Morton

Co-Chairman, Eurotunnel

As often before in our seven-year partnership, André Bénard's words have captured the essential spirit of a great enterprise, the grandest European project of the 20th century.

It is done, and we who were there at the doing of it – in the engineering offices, on the sites, under the sea, among the bankers worldwide and in the ministries of both countries – can now look back and wonder that it got done. As Drake wrote to Sir Francis Walsingham in 1587, 'There must be a beginning of any great matter, but the continuing unto the end until it be thoroughly finished yields the true glory.'

The complexity of the task and conflicts structured into the project at the outset brought client, contractor and bankers into strong dispute at times about who was to pay for what. Soon, I believe, that memory will no longer cloud the project.

I was at the first undersea breakthrough, and stepped from England to France. There are other moments which I recollect and savour as I write. One was on 28 June 1991 when the last of the huge tunnel boring machines completed the breakthrough of the last tunnel, close to the median line. There were about two hundred wildly excited folk cheering down there, but to me it suddenly seemed totally silent: 'all the machines are silent', like the heavy guns after a battle.

Before that, on 16 November 1987, the moment in a crowded room in London when we signed the equity underwriting agreement. In Paris and London we had raised £770 million despite promising no dividend for a decade, and this was less than four weeks after Black Monday on the world's exchanges. The project was alive.

And then, on 12 March 1993, when a very ordinary but full-size French train behind a diesel locomotive glided without fuss between the platforms of our Folkestone terminal. The first 'train now arriving from Calais' had arrived – a quite extraordinary moment.

It is done, and there are thousands of people in TML, Eurotunnel and beyond who did it.

The final breakthrough, 28 June 1991: 'all the machines are silent'. *(From left to right)*: André Bénard, Pierre Matheron (TML Construction Director, France), Alastair Morton, and Philippe Essig (TML Chairman).

Photographers working for Eurotunnel and Transmanche Link have taken, at the latest estimate, 120,000 photographs of the construction and commissioning of the Channel Tunnel. More than 600 of these are printed here. They have been chosen to tell the story of the project from its beginnings in 1985 to its completion at the end of 1993. The brief captions have been written for general readers, avoiding technical terms where possible.

The book is chronological. After an initial description of the system and an account of the historical background, chapters cover periods of six months and present the major aspects of the project in a set sequence. English tunnels (the longer section of the tunnelling) are followed by French; the French terminal (the larger of the two) is followed by the English terminal. In the later chapters these four are followed by a section on the locomotives and wagons built to run through the tunnel. Chronological treatment proved unsuitable for minor topics, which are therefore grouped in sections within the chapters and listed on the contents page.

Readers wishing for fuller details of the construction should contact the Eurotunnel Exhibition Centre at Folkestone, whose address is given on the last page. There are already many technical publications about the Tunnel, and more will certainly follow. Given the space available in this book, we have made no attempt to cover technical questions in depth or systematically. For example, there were many minor differences in the construction techniques used on the French and English sides which are not shown.

Few people were privileged to see this great Anglo-French engineering project with their own eyes. Our hope is that these photographs will recapture something of the scale and atmosphere of the works, now that the miners have gone for ever and the sites are landscaped over. As these words are written, trains are already running through the tunnels in the final stages of commissioning. The next chapter in the history of the Channel Tunnels is yours to share.

Jeremy Wilson and Jérôme Spick

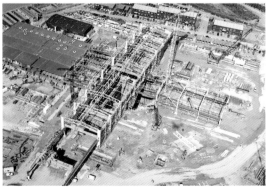

Anatomy of the Channel Tunnel

Except near the French coast, the Channel Tunnel was bored in a layer of chalk marl, which is a relatively soft yet impermeable rock. The three parallel tunnels are 50 km long and run at an average depth of 45 m beneath the seabed. Each of the outer pair, which are 7.6 m in diameter, contains a single one-way rail track. The service tunnel in the centre, 4.8 m in diameter, is for ventilation and maintenance, and can be used as a safe haven in an emergency. All three tunnels are linked by cross passages every 375 m, while piston-relief ducts between the rail tunnels arch over the service tunnel every 250 m. These ducts are designed to reduce the build up of pressure in front of advancing trains.

Long tunnels are almost always bored from both ends. This can halve the construction time and shortens the maximum distance that spoil, lining materials and workforce have to travel as the face advances. Engineers always try to avoid unnecessarily long headings, which make it more difficult to provide good ventilation and safe working conditions.

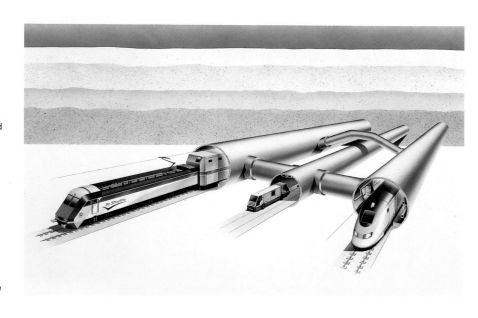

① Shakespeare Cliff - Construction Adit

② Sangatte Shaft

③ White and Grey Chalk

④ Chalk Marl

⑤ Gault Clay

⑥ Green Sand

⑦ Holywell Cut and Cover

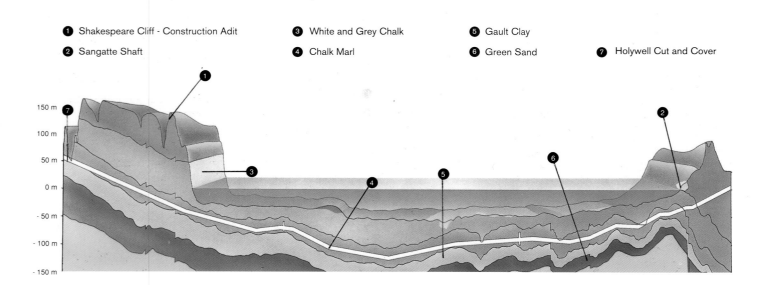

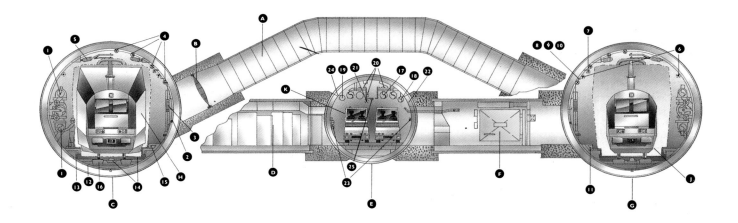

A Piston relief duct at 250 m intervals

B Piston relief damper

C North rail tunnel

D Typical technical room

E Service tunnel

F Typical cross-passage with bulkhead door

G Southern rail tunnel

H Shuttle

J Through train

K Service-tunnel transport system

RAIL TUNNELS

1 Cooling water pipes flow and return

2 Firemain (125 m each side of cross-passage)

3 Catenary tensioning weight (2 every 1.2 km)

4 Tensioning weight pulleys every 1.2 km

5 Catenary equipment (every 27 m)

6 Leaky feeder

7 Main lighting

8 2 x 20 KV cables

9 1 x 3 KV cable

10 Low-voltage cables

11 Signalling cables

12 Phase 1 track concrete and drainage

13 Walkway concrete

14 Phase 2 trackbase concrete

15 Precast walkway units

16 Track blocks

SERVICE TUNNEL

17 Drainage pipes

18 Firemain

19 Firemain (future)

20 20 KV/3.3 KV & other supply cables

21 Leaky feeders

22 Control & communications cables

23 Main lighting push buttons (both sides)

24 Loudspeakers (both sides)

25 Main lighting

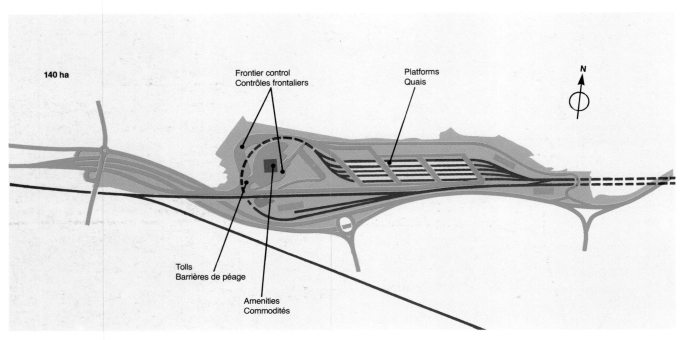

140 ha

Frontier control
Contrôles frontaliers

Platforms
Quais

N

Tolls
Barrières de péage

Amenities
Commodités

Plan of the Folkestone terminal

*The Channel Tunnel is designed
for through-trains and a
shuttle service for vehicles. These
board at the two terminals.*

Road vehicles passing through the Channel
Tunnel board and leave the giant shuttle
trains at terminals beside the M20 motorway at Folkestone and the A16 autoroute
near Calais. Passenger and freight through-
trains do not stop at these terminals. They
have direct access to the Tunnel via railway
links with the national rail networks.

The terminals provide a simple and
efficient interface between the motorway
(or local roads) and the shuttle service
through the Tunnel. In this respect, the terminals fulfil exactly the same function,
although they are very different in size. A
600 hectare site was available in France
compared to only 140 hectares in England.

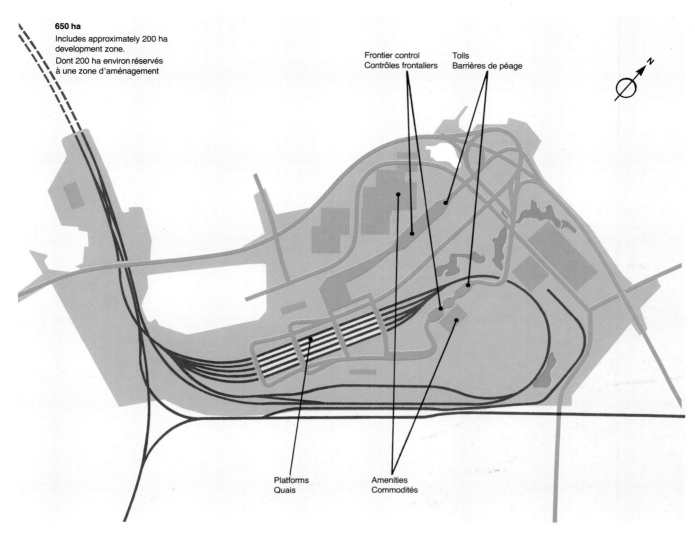

Frontier control
Contrôles frontaliers

Tolls
Barrières de péage

Platforms
Quais

Amenities
Commodités

Plan of the Calais terminal

At each terminal the shuttles turn round on a semicircular loop track before reaching the platform area. There are separate shuttles for freight vehicles and tourist vehicles such as cars, coaches and motor cycles. The two categories of traffic follow separate routes through the terminals, passing through their own sets of tollbooths as well as British and French frontier controls before reaching the platform area. On arrival there are no further controls: the exit road from the platform area leads straight to the motorway. There are also passenger-service buildings on the terminals offering restaurants, shops and duty-free goods, as well as Exhibition Centres explaining the tunnel system. Other buildings, notably on the French side, house offices and maintenance facilities. Also in France, 185 hectares are set aside for development including a major commercial and leisure centre known as the Cité de l'Europe.

CHAPTER 1

Background to the Eurotunnel Project

The first known project for a tunnel under the English Channel, shown here, was put forward in 1802 by the French mining engineer Albert Mathieu. From the 1830s such schemes gained impetus through the efforts of another French engineer, Aimé Thomé de Gamond. He made the first geological and hydrographical surveys of the route and tried to promote a succession of projects. He even took these ideas to Napoleon III and Prince Albert, husband of Queen Victoria. After 1867 he was joined by a number of British promoters, notably William Low and Sir John Clarke Hawkshaw, but for a variety of reasons none of their proposals came to fruition.

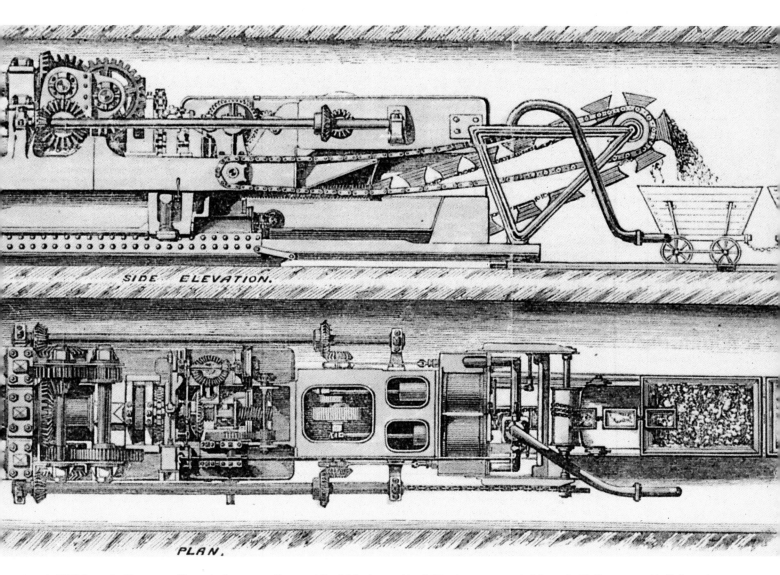

SIDE ELEVATION.

PLAN.

In 1876 the project for a cross-Channel railway tunnel led to an official Anglo-French protocol, and in 1881 a British railway entrepreneur, Sir William Watkin, began exploratory work at Shakespeare Cliff near Dover. His Anglo-French Submarine Railway Company was associated with a French group which included Alexandre Lavalley, contractor for the Suez Canal. Using a Beaumont-English boring machine 2.13 m in diameter, a pilot tunnel 1893 m long was bored from Shakespeare Cliff. In France, where a similar machine was used, 1669 m were excavated from a starting-point at Sangatte, west of Calais. The success of these experiments aroused furious opposition among influential military and political figures in Britain, who mounted a campaign against the project in the press and in Parliament. They argued that a tunnel would be a fatal weakness in Britain's national defences. In May 1882 they triumphed, and the project was abandoned.

Despite the enthusiasm of the pro-tunnel lobby during the first half of the 20th century, critics among Britain's military advisers retained the upper hand. Attempts to revive the project were all rejected. It was not until 1955 that the British government officially accepted that such arguments had lost their force. Any future war would be determined by air power. Thereafter, the debate about a fixed link across the Channel focused on engineering and economic questions. The British and French governments supported detailed technical and geological studies which led finally, in 1974, to the beginning of construction work on both sides of the Channel. This scheme, dependent on government finance, followed the long-favoured principle of twin rail tunnels on either side of a smaller service tunnel. In order to maximise revenue, the tunnel system was designed both for conventional railway traffic and for large shuttle wagons which would provide a 'rolling motorway' for road vehicles.

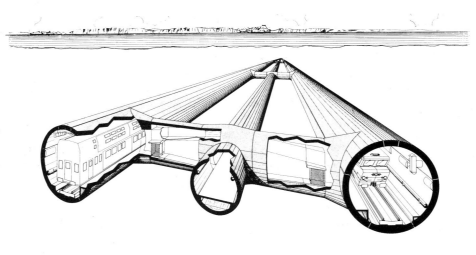

The French starting point would be at Sangatte, west of Calais. The sloping access tunnel was not completed by the end of 1974, but the service-tunnel boring machine had been delivered.

The English starting-point for the undersea tunnels would be Shakespeare Cliff, as in the 1881 scheme. This photograph shows preparatory work taking place on the land platform created in 1842, when a large section of cliff was blasted away during work on the railway line between Folkestone and Dover. The three undersea tunnels bored from this point would be linked by landward tunnels to the terminal site at Cheriton on the northern outskirts of Folkestone.

While the first English tunnel boring machine, seen here, was being built, major changes were taking place in British politics. Parliamentary elections in October 1974 brought the Labour Party to power with a small majority. The new government, uncertain even about Britain's continued membership of the EC, viewed the tunnel with far less enthusiasm than Edward Heath's Conservatives. Moreover, the project now included high-speed rail links to both London and Paris. By the end of 1974 cost estimates for the London link had risen by some 200 per cent at a time when the national economy faced mounting problems on several fronts. In January 1975, to the utter dismay of its French partners, the British government withdrew from the project. By then, the boring machine for the British undersea service tunnel was ready to start up.

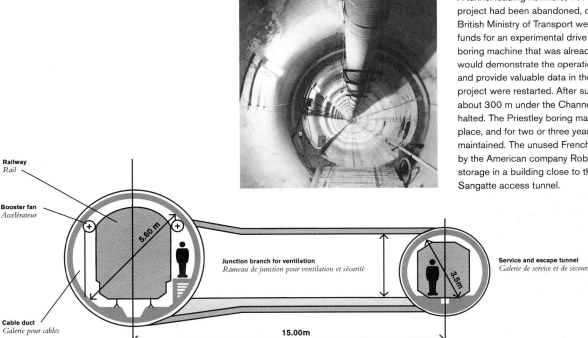

A tunnel leading nowhere, 1975. Although the project had been abandoned, officials at the British Ministry of Transport were able to obtain funds for an experimental drive with the tunnel boring machine that was already in place. This would demonstrate the operation of the machine and provide valuable data in the event that the project were restarted. After successfully driving about 300 m under the Channel, work was halted. The Priestley boring machine remained in place, and for two or three years was regularly maintained. The unused French machine, made by the American company Robbins, was put in storage in a building close to the entrance to the Sangatte access tunnel.

Railway
Rail

Booster fan
Accélérateur

5.60 m

Junction branch for ventilation
Rameau de junction pour ventilation et sécurité

3.5m

Service and escape tunnel
Galerie de service et de secours

Cable duct
Galerie pour cables

15.00m

The Mousehole Project, 1979. There seemed no hope of reviving the project during the life of the British Labour government. However, when the Conservatives returned to power in 1979, the British and French Railways soon made it known that they were working on a relatively low-cost scheme which might be expanded in stages. The first step would be to build a service tunnel and single rail tunnel which would be used alternately by groups of trains travelling from England to France and vice-versa. There would be no road-

vehicle shuttle, and hence no need for extensive terminals. Some dubbed this small-bore tunnel scheme 'The Mousehole', although it undoubtedly had merits. In the event, the new British cabinet was deeply committed to the cuts in government spending and saw no merit in funding the railway project. Yet the Prime Minister, Margaret Thatcher, made it clear that she would have no objection to a tunnel or other form of fixed cross-Channel link provided it could be financed from non-Government sources. At a summit meeting in

1981 between Mrs Thatcher and the French President, François Mitterrand, the two leaders agreed to set up an official working group which would examine the question. This initiative led to a series of technical and financial studies and to the development of tunnel and bridge schemes by different engineering groups. Finally, in April 1985, the British and French governments issued a formal Invitation to Promoters to submit schemes for a fixed link. The closing date for submissions was midnight on 31 October.

The Channel Tunnel Group/France-Manche submission, consisting of eleven volumes plus maps, had to be presented in exactly parallel English and French editions. This outline of a highly complex project had been prepared in only seven months, and it is said that during the final three weeks there were ten thousand amendments. The proposal was, nevertheless, a very convincing document. Both the civil engineering and the transport system were based on tried and tested technologies, while the design drew strength from development work carried out for the project abandoned in 1975. The environmental impact assessment, a requirement under EC law then in draft, was particularly substantial.

In all there were nine submissions, and the CTG/F-M scheme was among the four shortlisted. The other three all offered a drive-through link with the possibility of separate railway services. They

In England a group of major construction companies had jointly developed a new scheme along the lines of the project abandoned in 1975. Known as the Channel Tunnel Group, or CTG, these companies now included two banks. The group members were: Balfour Beatty Construction, Costain UK, Tarmac Construction, Taylor Woodrow Construction, George Wimpey International, National Westminster Bank and Midland Bank. French companies were extremely interested in the fixed-link project, but there was no single equivalent grouping. As the British and French governments were likely to favour proposals from an Anglo-French consortium, a group called France-Manche was now formed in France by five construction companies and three banks. They were Bouygues, Dumez, the Société Auxiliaire d'Entreprises, the Société Générale d'Entreprises Sainrapt et Brice, Spie Batignolles, Banque Nationale de Paris, Crédit Lyonnais, and Banque Indosuez.

The role of the banks in these groups was to advise on methods by which the scheme could be financed, and to secure vital loan commitments in support of the proposal. On 2 July 1985 the two sides met to form the Anglo-French consortium (referred to in short as CTG/F-M). This photograph of the occasion shows *(seated, centre)* Sir Nicholas Henderson, Chairman of CTG, signing the formal agreement with Jean-Paul Parayre, Chairman of France-Manche. At the rear are Philippe Montagnier, then General Manager of France-Manche, and Michael Gordon, Managing Director of CTG.

Protesters outside the Houses of Parliament. One of the submissions entered on 31 October was opposed to any kind of fixed link. This was part of an extremely energetic publicity campaign mounted under the name 'Flexilink' by those involved in the cross-Channel ferry industry. There had been no equivalent campaign in 1974, when the French and British governments had been partners in the tunnel project. At that time Sealink, one of the largest ferry operators, had been state-owned.

By 1985 the ferry companies, which were mainly British, were private operators and so were entitled to defend their commercial interests. To the puzzlement of many overseas observers, Flexilink continued to rouse British opinion against this immense binational project throughout 1986 and 1987.

were: Eurobridge, a suspension bridge with spans 4.5 km long supporting a motorway enclosed in a tube; Euroroute, a 21 km tunnel between artificial islands approached from each coast by bridges; and Channel Expressway, which had large-diameter road tunnels with embedded rail tracks and two mid-Channel ventilation towers.

Despite the attractions of the rival projects and the credibility of their sponsors, the award went to the Channel Tunnel Group and France-Manche.

The governments' choice is announced, January 1986. Successive engineering and financial studies had shown that the CTG/F-M project was probably the only practicable scheme. Yet many politicians would have preferred something more dramatic and innovative. In 1984 Margaret Thatcher had looked forward to 'a project which can show visibly how the technology of this age has moved to link the Continent and Britain closer together'. Public opinion, for its part, was strongly in favour of a drive-through link. By 20 January 1986, when President Mitterrand and Margaret Thatcher met at Lille to announce the choice made by the two governments, the outcome seemed far from certain.

Despite the attractions of the rival projects and the credibility of their sponsors, the award went to the Channel Tunnel Group and France-Manche. Even in the more conventional schemes, technology was unable to overcome the enormous difficulties posed by a drive-through link. Among these were the problems of safe tunnel ventilation, of measures to deal with the consequences of traffic accidents, and the probability that many drivers would become mesmerised in a tunnel of this length.

The seven-month interval since the submission meant that most of those seconded by partner-companies to work on the proposal had returned to work on other projects. Yet the challenge had been won. In the words of a press release 'an immense amount of hard work is now required to meet the Parliamentary timetable, to complete the detailed design work, and to raise the huge sums of money required to finance the project in order to enable construction to commence in the summer of 1987'.

The design and future construction work would be carried out by the ten construction companies in the CTG/F-M group. The five French companies formed a joint-venture group called GIE Transmanche Construction, which would build the French terminal and the tunnels from Sangatte.

The parallel grouping in England was called Translink Joint Venture. It would build the UK terminal and the tunnels from Shakespeare Cliff. The two national partnerships were linked in a binational project organisation called Transmanche-Link, or TML.

In France, where there is a long tradition of investment in major infrastructure projects, the Channel Tunnel met with widespread approval. In April 1987 the French National Assembly voted unanimously in favour of the legislation. Nevertheless, much work was needed to complete the legislative process. The massive document shown here was part of the preparation for the public inquiry which led to the Déclaration d'Utilité Publique in May. At the beginning of June the French Senate in turn gave its unanimous support.

Another demanding task during this period was the acquisition of land, notably on the terminal site. This was achieved in record time.

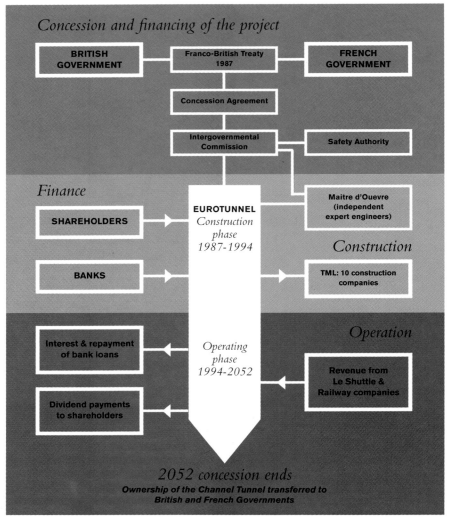

Concession and financing of the project

In Britain the legislative process included detailed examination by select committees of the House of Commons and the House of Lords. The House of Commons select committee is seen here making history by holding some of its hearings in Kent rather than Westminster.

Eurotunnel also set up information offices in Folkestone and Calais where local people could learn about the project and discuss their concerns. This consultation played an important part in gaining local acceptance, particularly in Kent.

In February 1987 the third reading of the Channel Tunnel Bill was carried in the House of Commons by 94 votes to 22. The bill then passed to the House of Lords. In June progress was interrupted by a general election, but the Channel Tunnel Act finally passed into British law in late July.

TML was to design and build the Channel Tunnel but, in order to pay for the work, a separate legal entity had to be established: a private company which would raise the necessary finance through equity and loans. To make that possible, the British and French governments would award the new company a 55-year operating concession (later extended to 65 years). The profits from this would be used to repay the loans and pay dividends to shareholders.

To fulfil this requirement a new Anglo-French organisation called Eurotunnel was formed. It absorbed CTG/F-M (to whom the governments had awarded the project) and signed a construction contract with TML.

While the terms of the Concession agreed in March 1986 gave Eurotunnel commercial

freedom to operate the system until 2042, the British and French governments retained the final decision on engineering and safety matters. Thus the design, construction, and testing of the system had to be approved by an expert Intergovernmental Commission assisted by a highly qualified Safety Authority. The Intergovernmental Commission would need to be satisfied before it granted Eurotunnel an Operating Certificate.

Raising finance
on an unprecedented scale.

One of the French
advertisements to
potential share-
holders, 1987.

Alastair Morton,
British co-Chairman of
Eurotunnel, addresses
dignitaries and the
press during a stop on
the Eurotunnel
Roadshow.

The private funding of such a large infra-structure project without recourse to government financial guarantees was a complex operation of unprecedented scale. The CTG/F-M partners subscribed an initial equity of £46 million in September 1986. This was increased by a £206 million private institutional placement that October. In November 1987 a public share offer raised a further £770 million from investors in France, Britain and several other countries. Just before this, a syndicated bank loan and letter of credit facility had been arranged for funds totalling £5 billion. The public share offer was promoted in Britain through a Shareholder Information Office in London and a travelling roadshow, as well as through press and television advertisements. There was also a press and television campaign in France.

A vital element in the financing was a Railway Usage Agreement signed between Eurotunnel, British Rail and SNCF. This gave Eurotunnel guaranteed future revenue in exchange for use by the railways of half the tunnel capacity.

CHAPTER 2

July 1986 – June 1987

1986
1 September:

Equity I - The Channel Tunnel consortium partners complete subscription of £46 million for the project.

25 September:

André Bénard appointed French Co-Chairman of Eurotunnel in succession to Jean-Paul Parayre.

29 October:

Equity II: Eurotunnel raises a further £206 million through a private institutional equity placement.

1987
20 February:

Alastair Morton appointed English Co-Chairman of Eurotunnel in succession to Lord Pennock, who had himself succeeded Sir Nicholas Henderson.

2 February:

Channel Tunnel Bill passes its third reading in the House of Commons.

23 March:

10,000th visitor to Eurotunnel roadshow train.

22 April:

French National Assembly unanimously approves Channel Tunnel legislation.

12 May:

The European Investment Bank agrees to lend £1 billion for the Channel Tunnel project.

4 June:

French Senate unanimously approves Channel Tunnel Legislation.

15 June:

French Channel Tunnel legislation signed by President Mitterrand.

It had been hoped that after March 1986, when the Channel Tunnel Concession was signed, it would be possible to make a start on major works. In the event, however, authorities on the British side were unwilling to grant the necessary permissions until parliamentary legislation was complete. In France, by contrast, work

In both countries, the legislative process called for reports, technical documents, and widespread consultation.

soon began on a huge access shaft, large enough to contain the Arc de Triomphe.

Despite this hold-up on the English side, there was plenty to do. In both countries, the legislative process called for reports, technical documents, and widespread consultation. It was also necessary to carry out all the administrative steps required at a local level, for example applying for planning consent for temporary and permanent roads and buildings.

While the outline design of the tunnels and transport system had been established, TML now faced the major task of developing the detailed design and the construction programme. This involved taking large numbers of decisions

about complex questions such as the optimum diameters of the tunnels. Answers could only be reached after investigation and, frequently, a programme of tests at a specialist research institute. The chosen design had then to pass through a highly structured procedure. In particular, detailed proposals agreed between TML and Eurotunnel had to be submitted for approval by the Intergovernmental Commission (IGC) and its specialist Safety Authority. The proposals and works were also studied at every stage by the Maître d'Oeuvre, a group of expert engineers from W. S. Atkins in England and Setec in France. Their independent conclusions were reported to Eurotunnel and the IGC.

While Eurotunnel set about raising finance and negotiating the terms of a usage agreement for trains belonging to the French and British railways, TML had to recruit a large staff, establish its organisation and procedures, and begin a colossal programme of procurement.

In December 1986 a jack-up rig off Shakespeare Cliff began work on ten boreholes for a geo-technical study of the area. Later, a sea wall would be built here to protect an enlarged land platform made from tunnel spoil. Meanwhile, the cross-Channel surveys developed for the 1974–5 tunnel project were refined using the latest satellite obser-vations. In liaison with the French and British authorities, TML pro-duced definitive surveys for the tunnel construction.

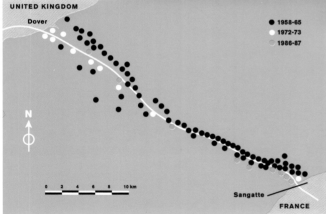

Geological studies for a Channel tunnel began in the 19th century, but the first exploration using modern methods took place in the 1950s. Investigations in 1964–5 and 1972–3 provided data from a hundred boreholes and established the best alignment for a tunnel. In 1986–7, needing further information, TML hired two large offshore rigs and drilled twelve more 180 m boreholes. These cost about £500,000 each.

An unexpected difficulty. For the first years after its experi-mental drive, the 1975 tunnel boring machine (TBM) had been main-tained in case the project was revived. Finally, to save cost, it was dismantled and removed. The cutter-head was left behind, entombed in a con-crete plug, as a buttress for the work-ing face. The plug should have been made with a weak con-crete mix, but it turned out to be very hard indeed!

Shakespeare Cliff, future construction site for the English tunnel workings, in December 1986. As in the 1974–5 tunnel scheme, the land-platform at the foot of the cliff would be used as pithead for the underground workings.

One legacy from 1974 was a road tunnel leading down to the platform from the clifftop. The lower entrance, approached by a ramp, is clearly visible. During the construction works temporary site offices would be built in the Aycliffe Valley to the left of the picture.

The railway along the foot of Shakespeare Cliff was a major asset. At the peak of the construction operations, trains would deliver 7,500 tonnes of materials to the site every 24 hours.

Another legacy from 1974 was the stack of concrete tunnel-lining segments. As the dimensions had changed they could not be used. They were thrown into the sea, to be buried under tunnel spoil when the platform was enlarged.

Though regularly inspected, the underground workings at Lower Shakespeare Cliff had been closed off for twelve years. During 1986–7, while Parliamentary legislation was in progress, the British Ministry of Transport gave permission for some preparatory work. The major task was to remove the remains of the 1975 TBM.

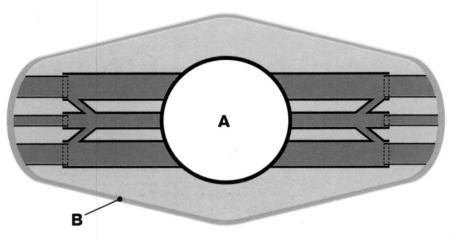

The Sangatte shaft was excavated inside a membrane of watertight material, drilled from the surface and reaching down to impermeable rock 42 m below sea level. This created an elliptical area 200 x 100 m which was isolated from the surrounding land. As a result, the shaft required little pumping and the works did not affect the local ground water, an important supply source for communities nearby.

A Sangatte shaft and initial galleries excavated before the TBMs arrived
B Waterproof membrane

In March 1987 work was in full swing a few hundred metres from the sea at Sangatte. A giant shaft, 55 m across and 65 m deep, was being excavated so that tunnelling could begin 30 m below sea level. The faint elliptical line in the soil around the head of the shaft is the only visible trace of the watertight membrane put in place during January and February.

After digging 12 m, excavators had to demolish the ramp used by lorries carrying away spoil. Thereafter, the spoil was lifted out in skips like the one on the left, each holding about 20 tonnes. The upper walls of the shaft had been cast beforehand, working from the surface.

Early 1987: at Sangatte a shaft was opened up as the first step in the excavation of the French Tunnels.

In June 1987 the shaft floor reached the level of the tunnels, a chalk stratum some 30 m below sea level. Holes in the shaft walls show where the construction-railway marshalling areas at the entrance to each tunnel would be excavated. Much of this excavation would be completed before further work on the lowest section of the shaft.

Roadheaders similar to this machine, seen opening up one of the marshalling areas, played a vital role. Unlike the tunnel boring machines, they were highly manoeuvrable and could carve out tunnels to any required dimension in the soft rock.

23 July:

The Channel Tunnel Act receives Royal Assent.

29 July:

The French and British leaders exchange the instruments of ratification of the Franco-British Channel Fixed Link Treaty.

29 July:

The Rail Usage Agreement is signed between Eurotunnel, British Rail and SNCF.

9 October:

The French government announces the construction of the TGV Nord which will link the Tunnel with Paris.

October:

Eurotunnel Exhibition Centre opens, overlooking the Sangatte site.

4 November:

Bank Credit Agreement signed between Eurotunnel and a worldwide syndicate of banks, providing a loan and letter of credit facility of £5 billion.

7 November:

The first segment train leaves the Isle of Grain.

27 November:

Equity III - Eurotunnel completes its public equity placing, raising an additional £770 million.

30 November:

Raymond Barre visits French sites.

CHAPTER 3

July – November 1987

Once the Channel Tunnel legislation was complete, work began on the English side to create access for tunnel-boring equipment. Within weeks, activity at Shakespeare Cliff was as hectic as it was at Sangatte. At the end of September direct TML employees numbered 1,100 in France and 1,500 in England, and the consortium had placed orders worth over £300 million.

London rather than Paris and Lyon.

On the British side, there were no immediate plans for a high-speed line. The existing track between Folkestone and London was to be renewed before the Tunnel opened, and this would be sufficient for services in the first few years.

> *At the end of September direct TML employees numbered 1,100 in France and 1,500 in England, and the consortium had placed orders worth over £300 million.*

In early October, the French government announced its decision to build a new high-speed railway line between Paris and the Channel Tunnel. This was a major boost to the Eurotunnel project, since reduced journey times for passenger trains between London and Paris would help the railways compete with airlines on this route, one of the busiest in Europe. Such a line had been part of the 1974-5 project. Had that not been abandoned, the first TGVs would have run between Paris and

The express service between Victoria Station and Gatwick Airport had demonstrated that it was possible to run frequent fast trains on the same track as local and commuter traffic into London. In the longer term, as most people recognised, a high-speed line would be necessary. Otherwise, priority given to the growing international passenger and freight traffic would completely paralyse other rail services in Kent.

News of the TGV Nord helped Eurotunnel to raise finance and by the end of November the funds required were in place.

A roadheader and the 'New Austrian Tunnelling Method' (NATM) were used to build a second access adit from Lower Shakespeare Cliff to the underground works. This larger adit, christened 'A2', was 12 m wide. Work began in November 1987 and was completed in May 1988. Also visible *(top left)* is the entrance to the 1974 road tunnel to Upper Shakespeare Cliff.

NATM was developed in the late 1950s and can be much faster than traditional methods. The initial tunnel lining is created by spraying a layer of quick-setting concrete ('shotcrete'), usually onto a steel-mesh reinforcement.

The new undersea service-tunnel TBM, brought in small sections from the pithead, would soon be assembled in this undersea chamber. Meanwhile, TML was putting in place the infrastructure needed for tunnelling: a construction railway, power supply, ventilation equipment, pumps, equipment for removing spoil, and a supply of tunnel-lining segments.

In the late summer of 1987, equipment and supplies for the tunnel workings began to accumulate at Lower Shakespeare Cliff. Among the rolling stock seen on the first narrow-gauge tracks of the construction railway are three locomotives, fitted with rack-and-pinion drives so that they could pull heavy loads up the 15% gradient in the access adit. Sections of the new service-tunnel TBM *(centre)* were waiting for transport underground.

Equipment began to assemble at Shakespeare Cliff in late 1987.

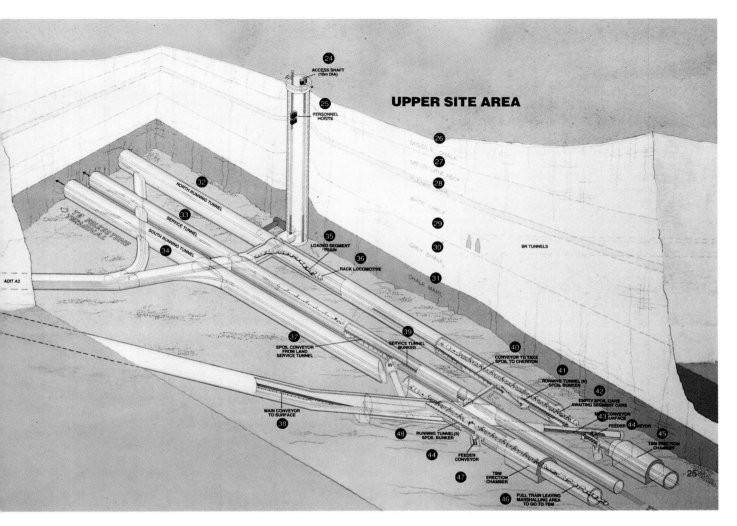

UPPER SITE AREA

1. 20 t high-speed gantry cranes
2. Loaded segment train
3. Tunnel-lining segment stacks
4. Unloading point for rail delivery of aggregates
5. Cement silos
6. 2 x 80 cu m/hr concrete batcher and cement silos
7. Aggregate stock piles
8. To upper Shakespeare Cliff
9. Portal to British Rail main line tunnels to Dover
10. Site access tunnel
11. Empty segment train
12. Entrance to Adit A2
13. Ventilation fans
14. Materials laboratory
15. Tunnel support equipment
16. BR tunnels
17. Adit A1
18. Plant stores
19. Locomotive workshops
20. Main spoil conveyor
21. Stand-by spoil
22. Access to seawall construction
23. Conveyor transfer station
24. Access shaft (10 m dia)
25. Personnel hoists
26. Middle chalk
27. Melbourne rock
28. Plenus marl
29. White chalk
30. Grey chalk
31. Chalk marl
32. North rail tunnel
33. Service tunnel
34. South rail tunnel
35. Loaded segment train
36. Rack and pinion locomotive
37. Spoil conveyor from land service tunnel
38. Main conveyor to surface
39. Service-tunnel bunker
40. Spoil conveyor
41. North rail tunnel
42. Empty spoil cars
43. Main conveyor to surface
44. Feeder conveyor
45. TBM erection chamber
46. Full train leaving marshalling area to go to TBM
47. TBM erection chamber
48. South rail tunnel spoil bunker

September: work starting on the marshalling area of the southern undersea rail tunnel *(left)*, while the service tunnel *(right)* was well advanced. First, the upper part of each tunnel was excavated and lined, then the lower part, beginning in the centre.

By mid-November the supporting framework was in place for a steel deck at the level of the tunnel floors. Work excavating the shaft to its final depth had begun in August and would be completed by the end of the year.

Four pillars, each 2 m in diameter, rose from the base of the shaft to support the steel deck. During the next five years, construction trains carrying millions of tonnes of spoil and tunnelling materials would pass above them.

CHAPTER 4

December 1987 - June 1988

1987
1 December:

Start of English undersea service-tunnel drive.

1988
27 January:

The French service-tunnel TBM arrives at Dunkirk.

1988
28 January:

François Mitterrand visits Sangatte.

5 February:

Margaret Thatcher visits Shakespeare Cliff tunnels and tries her hand driving the service tunnel TBM.

28 February:

Start of French undersea service-tunnel drive (T1).

End-March:

First kilometre of English undersea service-tunnel drive.

28 June:

Start of French landward service tunnel drive (T4).

By the end of February the first two tunnel boring machines were at work at each end of the undersea service tunnel. Further machines would shortly be delivered.

With finance in place, the uncertainties fanned by Flexilink and other opponents on the British side were swept

design contracts for the new high-speed international passenger trains. In mid-June, it published a study of its long-term requirements related to the Tunnel, short-listing four alternative routes that would cut the journey time between London and Paris to 2½ hours. Meanwhile the French

The prospect of completing the Tunnel turned attention to its consequences.

away. The project now had greater momentum than any of its predecessors.

The prospect of completing the Tunnel turned attention to its consequences. Alastair Morton began calling on the British government to take a fresh approach to infrastructure investment and to reconsider a high-speed rail link between London and the Tunnel. For its part, British Rail submitted plans for an International Station at London Waterloo and, with its continental partners, placed

government had announced plans to build a high-speed line round Paris linking the TGV Nord with lines to Strasbourg, Lyon, and the new TGV Atlantique.

By mid-summer the two undersea service-tunnel drives were both behind schedule because of teething problems and bad ground. TML engineers and the equipment manufacturers were working hard to find solutions to these difficulties. Happily, work on the terminals was going well.

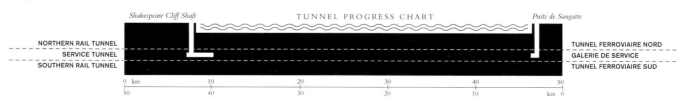

Shakespeare Cliff Shaft   TUNNEL PROGRESS CHART   Puits de Sangatte

NORTHERN RAIL TUNNEL		TUNNEL FERROVIAIRE NORD
SERVICE TUNNEL		GALERIE DE SERVICE
SOUTHERN RAIL TUNNEL		TUNNEL FERROVIAIRE SUD

0 km 10 20 30 40 50
50 40 30 20 10 km 0

The cutterhead of the TBM for the northern undersea rail-tunnel on the British side. Nearly 9 m in
diameter, it was already impressive with only four
of its eight pick-studded arms in place. In action,
the head could turn at 3.3 rpm with a thrust up to
4,220 tonnes.

How a tunnel boring machine works.

The teeth of the cutter-head were cutting picks or discs, armed with hardened steel. In the British tunnels, where the chalk was mainly dry, picks were used for preference. On French machines, the rock was broken up by disks then torn away from the face with picks.

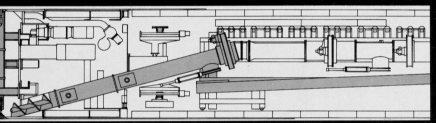

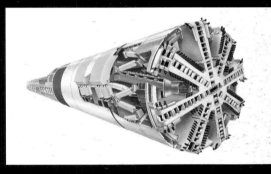

Three basic types of TBM were used on the Channel Tunnel project:

1 machines designed to work in open mode only, used for both landward and undersea tunnels on the UK side where dry conditions were expected;

2 machines designed for either open or closed mode, used for the French undersea tunnels which would pass through fissured water-bearing rock near the coast before reaching dry conditions;

3 TBMs designed to work in closed mode only, used for the short French landward tunnels where some of the ground would be wet.

In addition to these fundamental types, there were differences between machines ordered from the various makers, and between machines used for the service tunnel and the much larger rail tunnels.

The fastest TBMs were those designed to cut through dry rock. In these 'open mode' machines, the spoil conveyor belt began directly behind the cutterhead, and tunnel-lining segments were placed against the exposed rock surface at the rear of the TBM casing.

Machines on the French side, designed to pass through areas of wet ground, could operate in a much slower 'closed' mode. There was a water-tight bulkhead behind the cutterhead, through which spoil was carried by an Archimedes screw. The tunnel lining was built inside the TBM's cylindrical casing and sealed with grout before the machine moved forwards. In closed mode, the TBM was like a kind of submarine at the end of a dry, sealed tunnel.

The stratum of chalk marl through which the tunnels were bored has been described as the perfect tunnelling medium. A circular full-face cutterhead at the front of each TBM acted like an enormous grater. Fragments of chalk, scraped off the face, fell into a collection mechanism behind the cutters. From there, the spoil was transferred by a conveyor system into wagons waiting under the TBM back-up train. The TBMs were clad in a cylindrical steel skin up to the point where the permanent tunnel linings were installed.

The TBM head is thrust forward by a series of hydraulic rams, pushing either against a section locked in place by gripper pads *(shown in orange)* or against the completed tunnel lining at the rear.

A section of one of the French rail-tunnel TBM heads, viewed from behind. The shield and pipework at this point were telescopic. When the machine was working in open mode, hydraulic rams thrust the cutterhead forwards. The gripper section immediately behind it remained stationary while the crew built a ring of lining segments.

Changing one of the large cutting disks, weighing more than 20 kg, which was used to break up harder rock. In highly compacted ground it was sometimes necessary to renew these disks after only 500 m.

Inside the cutterhead of a French rail-tunnel TBM before washing down. Light maintenance was carried out daily, with a longer session each week. Once a month, the cutterheads were washed down to allow detailed inspection.

The excavated chalk was transported on conveyor belts along the back-up train to discharge points where it fell into spoil wagons on the construction railway beneath.

How spoil is removed.

While the TBM crew build a segment ring at the rear of one of the British rail-tunnel TBMs, the spoil conveyor *(top left)* carries chalk back from the cutterhead.

The trains which brought tunnel-lining segments to the TBM on flat cars carried spoil in high-sided muck wagons on their return journey to the Sangatte shaft or Shakespeare Cliff.

A giant Archimedes screw, more than 1m in diameter, waiting to be installed in one of the French rail-tunnel TBMs. The screw would move spoil through the watertight bulkhead behind the cutterhead.

The tunnel linings consisted of rings of segments made from a special reinforced concrete. In the English rail tunnels, shown here, rings consisted of eight segments plus a smaller key segment, while six segments plus a key were used in the service tunnel. In the French tunnels there were 5 segments plus key.

Key Segment
Clé

How the tunnel is lined.

TBM progress was often measured in terms of the number of rings built: 1.5 m per ring in the English tunnels, 1.4 m or 1.6 m per ring in France. Labelled segments to form a complete ring were assembled at Lower Shakespeare Cliff for transport to the British TBMs, and at Sangatte in France for the French TBMs.

Part of the back-up train of a French rail-tunnel TBM, seen here just after it had been assembled in the Sangatte shaft. While the back-up train was still in the shaft, segments were lowered directly onto the upper conveyor. In some TBMs, segments were moved to the build area by handling systems at a lower level.

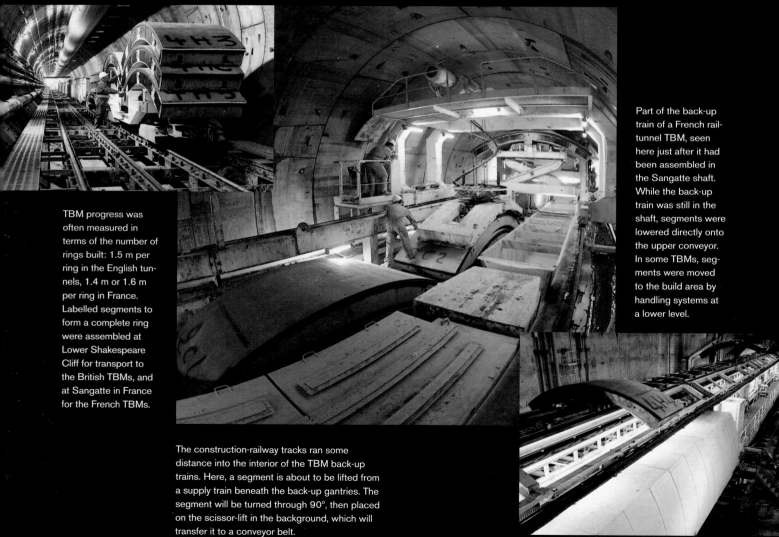

The construction-railway tracks ran some distance into the interior of the TBM back-up trains. Here, a segment is about to be lifted from a supply train beneath the back-up gantries. The segment will be turned through 90°, then placed on the scissor-lift in the background, which will transfer it to a conveyor belt.

The segment erecting crane of a British rail-tunnel TBM *(top)* has just placed a segment in position against the rock wall. Note the hydraulic rams in this picture taken from inside the TBM gripper section. When the ring is complete, the rams will press against it to push the gripper section forward, at the same time dragging along the back-up train .

In the French tunnels the gaps between segments were sealed with gaskets. Each new segment was therefore bolted to the adjacent ones.

Ring-building began with the lowest segment. On this English service-tunnel TBM, the three bottom segments were placed by crane. An arm, rotating through 180°, positioned the higher segments. The two English service-tunnel TBMs were very similar except that the bore was slightly larger in the landward tunnel to accommodate thicker segments.

Different types of grout were used in differing circumstances. Quick-setting varieties had to be mixed, just before use, under the TBM back-up train.

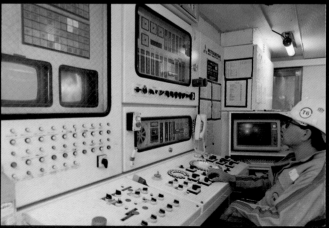

Left: Injecting grout through a segment. This process was carried out in all the tunnels, but in the French TBMs there was an additional void because segment rings were built inside the tail skin. As the TBM advanced, the tail skin left a gap around the outside of the ring, making it necessary to grout in several stages.

These enormous mechanical moles, containing around 700 motors and mechanisms, were controlled from consoles in a cabin near the front of the back-up train. The direction of bore was programmed in advance. If there was any divergence from the planned route, the driver could steer the machine using a system of hydraulic rams.

The laser beam passing through a 'gate' fixed to the tunnel wall.

Surveyors in the tunnels under Shakespeare Cliff. Survey teams at each end of the tunnel had to work with exceptional accuracy to ensure that the two undersea drives, starting 38 km apart, would meet. Alignments transferred from the surface to the tunnels at Sangatte and Shakespeare Cliff were related to the cross-Channel survey established through satellite observations of key points (the 'Réseau Trans-Manche 1987'). The survey network was then extended to a series of fixed points underground as the tunnels progressed.

Setting up a laser beam beside the TBM back-up train. The laser and the 'gates' through which its beam passed were mounted on precisely positioned brackets. The fixed beam therefore served as a reference line for the TBM's guidance system. It fell onto an electronic target attached to the TBM head, and the guidance system used its position on the target to compute any divergence between the actual TBM path and the planned trajectory.

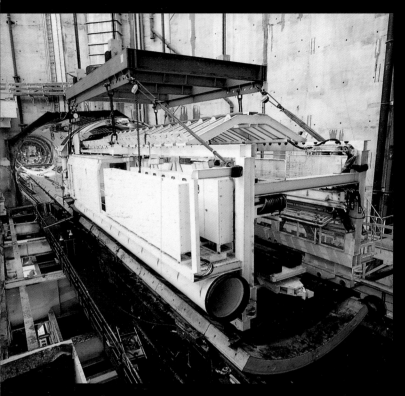

Below: The back-up train had to be washed continuously with a powerful hose to prevent the accumulation of mud. Although most of the spoil was carried away by the conveyor system, the small proportion left behind could rapidly amount to a considerable volume.

Above: The front section of the T5 back-up train being lowered into the Sangatte shaft. It would be joined to the TBM head, just visible in the marshalling area beyond. On the left, furthest from the camera, is the TBM control cabin, while the segment conveyor runs along the top.

The back-up trains in the rail tunnels had hollow centres wide enough for twin construction-railway tracks. In the service-tunnel TBMs, however, there was room for only one construction train. The tracks for the construction railway were laid near the front of the back-up train. In the English rail tunnels the track was laid on ballast, while in the service tunnel it was bolted to a concrete floor slab.

Huge ventilation ducts brought fresh air to the working face, pushing used air to the rear. Although the TBM was powered by electricity, the excavations produced heat and large amounts of dust.

Above: In the French tunnels the construction-railway track was mounted on steel girders. First, a cross-beam was secured to the segments, and then the track girders, identified with letters, were bolted into place. Sections of walkway filled the gaps between the rails, hiding the river of mud below. The right-hand photograph, looking back from the TBM head, also shows the track girder laid for the wheels of the back-up train.

Various start and finish dates have been published for the different drives because these events are hard to define. A TBM may 'first cut rock' during commissioning, but not begin its drive until two weeks later. The first completed segment ring, another significant start point, may be later still, since a full segment ring cannot be built until the TBM head has cleared the erection chamber.

As explained in chapter 10, when the undersea rail-tunnel drives met, the British TBMs built their final segment rings on the tunnel alignment and were then driven steeply downwards and buried clear of the tunnel path. Passing above them, the French machines took more than a day to complete the breakthrough.

The dates used here for the start of drives are those given in internal reports. Dates for the ends of drives are the date of the last segment ring built, or of a completed breakthrough.

A similar confusion exists about the length of drives. The distances given here are the total length of tunnel from fixed datum points at Shakespeare Cliff and the Sangatte Shaft. These may include the short initial sections of tunnel, where the TBMs were assembled, which had been excavated by other methods.

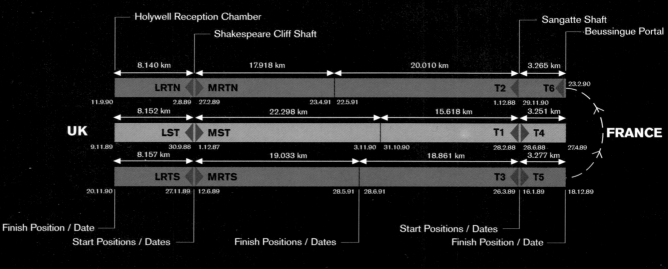

* The T5/T6 TBMs were the same machine. After driving the southern landward rail tunnel from Sangatte to the Beussingue portal, T5 was turned round and, as T6, drove the northern rail tunnel back to Sangatte.

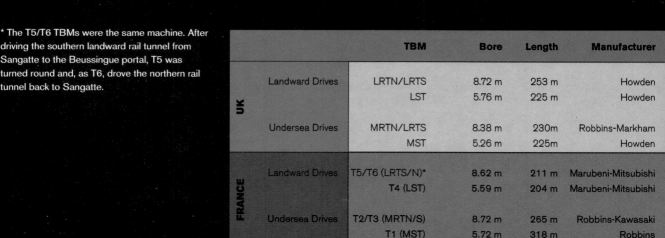

		TBM	Bore	Length	Manufacturer
UK	Landward Drives	LRTN/LRTS	8.72 m	253 m	Howden
		LST	5.76 m	225 m	Howden
	Undersea Drives	MRTN/LRTS	8.38 m	230m	Robbins-Markham
		MST	5.26 m	225m	Howden
FRANCE	Landward Drives	T5/T6 (LRTS/N)*	8.62 m	211 m	Marubeni-Mitsubishi
		T4 (LST)	5.59 m	204 m	Marubeni-Mitsubishi
	Undersea Drives	T2/T3 (MRTN/S)	8.72 m	265 m	Robbins-Kawasaki
		T1 (MST)	5.72 m	318 m	Robbins

The honour of starting the tunnel drives fell to the undersea service-tunnel TBM on the British side. The machine was built and tested by Howdens in Scotland, then dismantled for transport to Lower Shakespeare Cliff. In early October, when this photograph was taken, the head was being reassembled in the chamber where the 1975 tunnel had halted. A decision had meanwhile been taken to build the new tunnel to a slightly larger internal diameter than the 1975 tunnel: 4.8 m rather than 4.5 m. The existing 1975 section was not to be enlarged, so the back-up train for the new TBM, which began its drive on 1 December, could not be erected until a sufficient length of new tunnel had been bored.

In the first four months the British undersea service tunnel advanced 785 m, a reasonable performance during a start-up period before the main spoil conveyor was installed. As the TBM progressed, it laid a floor of concrete slabs which rested on ledges moulded into the lower segments at each side. The slabs would remain in the tunnel permanently, the space beneath them forming a drain.

By mid-February the first of the new sea walls at Lower Shakespeare Cliff was in place. The walls would create a series of enclosures to be filled with tunnel spoil. Much thought had been given to the destination of spoil from the British tunnels. Of all the sites examined, the best proved to be closest to the pithead. Research showed that the ecological effects of extending the existing land platform would be very slight, while the disturbance caused by transporting enormous volumes of spoil elsewhere might be considerable.

The new Adit A2 at Lower Shakespeare Cliff *(on the left)* was completed in the spring. It greatly improved access to the tunnels.

The 1974-5 excavations had helped speed the launch of the first British TBM, but the underground works at Lower Shakespeare Cliff needed considerable development before more machines could be assembled. Using roadheaders and conventional mining equipment, an initial section of each tunnel was excavated.

A large chamber had to be excavated where each of the four rail-tunnel TBMs would be assembled. This was done remarkably quickly, using the New Austrian Tunnelling Method for the primary linings. The steel mesh reinforcement sprayed with shotcrete can be seen in this view of the part-built chamber for the northern landward rail-tunnel TBM.

The first TBM for the French tunnels, shipped by sea from Portland in America, was unloaded at Dunkirk on 27 January 1988. It completed its journey to Sangatte by road.

Like its predecessor in 1975, the 470-tonne machine for the undersea service tunnel was designed and built by Robbins. This specialist company was also responsible, with Kawasaki in Japan and Markham in England, for all four TBMs used in the undersea rail tunnels.

The second French service-tunnel TBM, T4, was built by Marubeni-Mitsubishi. It would drive the landward tunnel from Sangatte to the future terminal. Using the 430-tonne overhead gantry crane mounted on rails across the top of the Sangatte shaft, it was lowered into position on 10–11 May 1988 at a gentle rate of 6 m per hour.

In a baptism ceremony on the shaft floor, TBM T4 was given the name Virginie. Its counterpart in the undersea service tunnel had been named Brigitte. Afterwards T4 was moved on rails to the far end of the landward service-tunnel marshalling area where, on 28 June, it would begin its drive.

In mid-March 1988 the main north–south hall of the shaft-head building was ready for its cladding. In the foreground are rings of tunnel-lining segments, each loaded onto a special carrier. In addition to the 430 tonne crane, there were two 60 tonne overhead gantry cranes in this hall for rail-tunnel segments. Service-tunnel segments were delivered to the east hall, where there was a 30 tonne gantry crane.

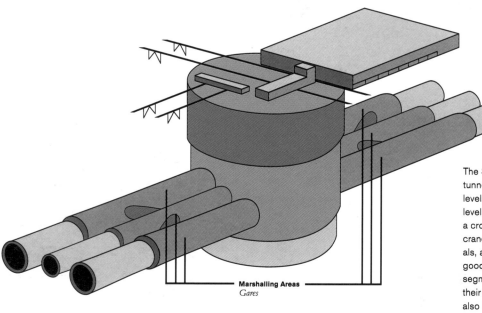

Marshalling Areas
Gares

The Sangatte shaft was at the heart of French tunnelling operations. There were four principal levels. The head of the shaft, 18 m above sea level, was roofed over by a building in the form of a cross. This sheltered the four overhead gantry cranes used to lower segments and other materials, as well as two personnel lifts and three goods lifts. At the level of the tunnels, -28 m, segments, materials and personnel set off for their destinations on construction trains which also brought spoil back from the TBMs. The lower levels, -43 m and -47 m, were used to convert the spoil to a chalky liquid, which was then pumped to the surface (see p.79).

The lower part of the lining in the marshalling areas was cast in sections. This work was completed in the second quarter of 1988, in readiness for delivery of the rail-tunnel TBMs.

At the beginning of 1988, when the shaft structure was complete, work began installing the five vats at -43 m where spoil would be mixed with water. Provisional arrangements were in place to dispose of spoil from the service-tunnel drives.

By mid-June 1988 the Sangatte construction site was taking shape. In the foreground are a buffer reservoir, stores, workshops and car parks; centre, to the rear, the cross-shaped building over the shaft; to the right, the segment factory and storage yard.

In the summer of 1988 the first stage of the Fond Pignon dam was completed. It had involved 570,000 cubic metres of earthworks. The top was 19 m high and 730 m long, and the space enclosed would hold 1.4 million cubic metres.

In August 1987 work began on the construction of a dam in the low hills behind the Sangatte shaft. The tunnel spoil would be mixed with water and pumped here, covering over an area dotted with shell craters and block-houses from the Second World War.

The first of the rail-tunnel TBMs – seen here being assembled at Dunkirk by Fives Cail Babcock – arrived by sea on 8 June. Following a request for tenders in the spring of 1987, it had been built in Japan by Kawasaki in association with Robbins.

Making segments to line the English tunnels.

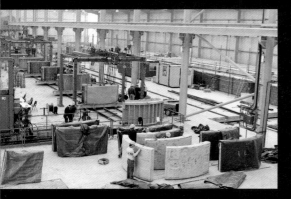

The first of eight production lines, October 1987. The line followed a rectangular path. In the foreground, segments emerging from the curing tunnel *(left)* were removed from their moulds and wrapped in thermal blankets to prevent them cooling too quickly. Further on, the empty moulds were fitted with a new reinforcement cage, then filled with concrete before entering the far end of the curing tunnel. The complete cycle took seven hours.

TML's Isle of Grain segment plant, May 1989. Peak production exceeded that of all other British precast factories put together.

In France the tunnel-lining segments were made in a factory on the Sangatte site. There was no space for such a plant at Lower Shakespeare Cliff, so segments had to be delivered by train.

As the crushed granite aggregate for the concrete was to come by sea from Scotland, TML built a factory on a site in northern Kent with deep water moorings and access to the rail network. This was on the Isle of Grain, which lies between the Rivers Thames and Medway. Production started in October 1987 and the first trainload was shipped to Shakespeare Cliff on 27 November. By June 1988 eight lines were producing over 1,000 units a day.

The plant, which produced 268 different shapes of segment, had excellent records for quality control and safety. In all, some 445,000 segments were made for the English tunnels, using 1,000,000 tonnes of aggregate, 200,000 tonnes of cement, and 44,500 tonnes of steel reinforcement. To increase the impermeability of the concrete, 90,000 tonnes of pulverised fuel ash were added to the mix. The segment concrete was the strongest ever produced, with almost twice the crushing strength of the concrete used in the pressure vessel of a nuclear reactor.

The last of 1,250 segment trains left for Shakespeare Cliff at the end of May 1991.

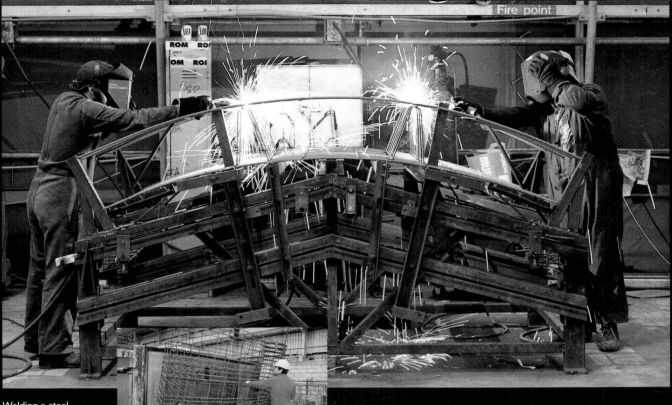

Welding a steel
reinforcement cage.

Guiding the reinforce-
ment cage into a mould.

A segment beginning
its five-hour progress
through the curing
tunnel.

After a minimum of four weeks in the storage
yard, segments were loaded into special trains
and shipped to Shakespeare Cliff. The trains
weighed up to 2,200 tonnes and took a
circuitous 158 km route to avoid steep gradients.

Rigorous quality
control at all stages
led to a very low reject
rate, which was all the
more remarkable
because the tolerance
for some dimensions
was as little as 0.1 mm.

Making segments to line the French tunnels.

Fewer types of segment were produced at Sangatte than the Isle of Grain. This made it possible to use highly automated equipment to make the reinforcement cages.

There was a fundamental difference between the British segments and those made at Sangatte for the French tunnels. While the British segments were intended for dry ground, the French segments needed watertight joints. They were therefore fitted with neoprene gaskets capable of resisting the maximum pressure that might be encountered. To maintain pressure on the gaskets during construction, the rings were bolted together. The fit between successive rings had to be perfect, even in places where the tunnel was changing direction. The solution was to make each ring very slightly narrower on one side than the other. When the tunnel was straight, the narrower side alternated. If the tunnel turned sideways, up, or down, the rings were installed with the narrower side on the inside of the curve. Because of this changing orientation, it was not possible to mould ledges into the segments, as was done on the English side.

Six segment-production lines used essentially the same carrousel principle as in England. Production began on 10 December 1987 and ended in the spring of 1991. A total of 252,000 segments was manufactured, with 72 different variants. In all, 425,000 tonnes of sand, 744,000 tonnes of aggregate, and 225,000 tonnes of cement were used to make 563,400 cubic metres of concrete. Most of these materials came from quarries near Boulogne and other sources in the region. The segments spent longer in curing tunnels than those in England, and therefore needed less time in the storage yard to reach their full strength. After a minimum of seven days they were ready for loading onto pallets, one ring at a time, and were then taken by special transporters to the head of the Sangatte shaft.

The Sangatte segment factory.

A segment production line. The mould carriers spent, on average, $14^1/_2$ minutes at each position. In all, 30,000 tonnes of steel were used for reinforcement cages. The specification required that the tunnel linings should last for at least 120 years, which is, in effect, indefinitely.

Pallets carrying complete rings waiting their turn to go down the shaft. They were moved around the site by self-propelled cranes resembling those used in yacht marinas. Details of every segment, from manufacture to final position in the tunnels, were logged by computer.

Fitting a neoprene gasket to a completed segment. As at the Isle of Grain, the segments had to pass rigorous quality control. To ensure an exact fit, the segments were made lying flat, with all four edges in the mould. Stress gauges were incorporated in selected segments throughout the tunnel system, so that the linings could be con-tinuously monitored.

The pallets were lowered down the Sangatte shaft by crane and then mounted on construction-railway bogies for the journey to the TBM.

One of the first tasks on the French terminal site was to drain the areas of marshland and consolidate them to a depth which varied from 3 m to as much as 18 m. After putting down a layer of porous sand with vertical and horizontal drains, a heavy surcharge of material was placed on top which would compress and compact the subsoil, much like squeezing water out of a sponge.

The future French tunnel portal would be at the bottom left-hand corner of this picture, at the lower end of a sloping trench leading up to the future terminal site *(back-ground, centre)*. By mid-1988 work on this 'Beussingue Trench' was well in hand.

Left: In England as in France, no alternative development had been permitted on the terminal sites identified for the 1970s scheme. However, on the British side, delay in obtaining access meant that only limited survey work was possible before the beginning of 1988. This view in October 1987 shows the terminal site before work began.

By the second quarter of 1988 the topsoil had been stripped and work was in hand on drainage and the first earthworks. Note Biggins Wood, a small area of ancient woodland in the middle of the site. Special measures were taken to conserve the plant species there.

Unearthing and preserving the past.

Stone Farm, one of four historic buildings which had to be removed to make way for work on the English terminal. These were carefully recorded and dismantled by the Canterbury Archaeological Trust for re-erection on other sites. Stone Farm was the most interesting building, containing substantial evidence of its 16th-century structure.

Between October 1987 and September 1988 thirty archaeologists helped by volunteers carried out systematic investigation of the French construction sites. They found and recorded ceramics, animal bones, weapons, jewels, and over 300 human skeletons. These showed that the area had been inhabited since Palaeolithic times.

On the English side, archaeological investigations were organised by the Canterbury Archaeological Trust. These included excavations at Ashford, Dover, the terminal, and at Holywell *(seen left),* where a rare Bronze-Age settlement was found, dating back 3,800 years.

CHAPTER 5

July – December 1988

July:

Eurotunnel Head Office moves to Victoria.

August:

Mock-up of a double-deck shuttle loading wagon tested at Ashford.

13 September:

Road bridge carrying the RN1 Calais-Boulogne road over the Beussingue trench is opened.

19 September:

Opening of the Eurotunnel Exhibition Centre, overlooking the English terminal site.

30 September:

Start of English landward service-tunnel drive.

1 December:

Start of French northern undersea rail-tunnel drive (T2).

15 December:

TML issues invitations to tender for shuttle locomotives and wagons.

During the late summer continuing difficulties with the undersea service tunnels were only partly offset by good progress in the French landward service-tunnel drive. By the spring, however, the French undersea tunnel would reach chalk marl. On the English side too, the TBM moved into dry ground and its progress began to exceed targets. Work on the terminal sites was could see the construction works. This obligation was met by Exhibition Centres at Sangatte and beside the English terminal. As the project progressed, both of these centres became enormously popular, particularly with children. On the English side there were frequent requests for teaching materials. This led Eurotunnel to join with the Kent Education Authority in setting up

At the end of the year five TBMs were in action 24 hours a day, and TML was directly employing 7,993 people. Eurotunnel staff numbered 580.

helped by unusually good weather during the autumn and early winter.

In November the funds raised through selling equity were exhausted. Eurotunnel therefore drew for the first time on its bank-loan facility.

The Channel Tunnel legislation had called for viewpoints where the public a department to develop and publish suitable titles. It soon built up an extensive list.

At the end of the year five TBMs were in action 24 hours a day, and TML was directly employing 7,993 people. Eurotunnel staff numbered 580. In addition, large numbers were employed by subcontractors on and off the sites.

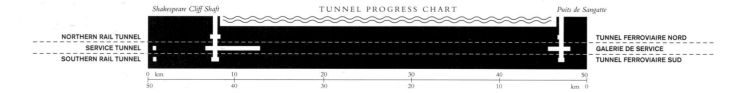

Shakespeare Cliff Shaft   TUNNEL PROGRESS CHART   Puits de Sangatte

NORTHERN RAIL TUNNEL — TUNNEL FERROVIAIRE NORD
SERVICE TUNNEL — GALERIE DE SERVICE
SOUTHERN RAIL TUNNEL — TUNNEL FERROVIAIRE SUD

The UK landward tunnels would be bored through ground where thicker segments were necessary. The TBMs used on the landward side therefore excavated a larger diameter than their undersea equivalents. This in turn meant that bigger chambers were needed to assemble them. The chamber shown here, for the northern landward rail tunnel, was completed by the end of 1988.

By October 1988 the upper and lower construction sites at Shakespeare Cliff were well established. Buildings on the upper site included offices, workshops, a medical centre and facilities for the tunnel workforce. Personnel lifts descending directly to the tunnels were to be installed in a 110 m ventilation shaft from this site. These would provide access for the work-force without interfering with the handling of materials at the Lower Shakespeare Cliff pithead. The top of the road tunnel to the lower site is just visible *(centre)*.

In France, the majority of construction work-ers were recruited from the local region. In England, a large part of the workforce came from other parts of Britain or Ireland. To reduce the demands on local accommodation, an encampment named 'Farthingloe village' was built to house 1,100 employ-ees. It included a shop, a sports hall and other leisure facilities. Seen here in October 1988, the village was opened in January 1989.

Installing support frames for overhead cranes in the chamber where one of the rail-tunnel TBMs would be assembled. The two caverns for the undersea tunnels involved 5,660 cubic metres of excavation, and visitors frequently compared them to cathedrals.

Part of the UK landward service-tunnel TBM on its way through the tunnel system at Lower Shakespeare Cliff. All six TBMs starting out from Shakespeare Cliff had to be transported in small pieces to the underground chambers where they were assembled.

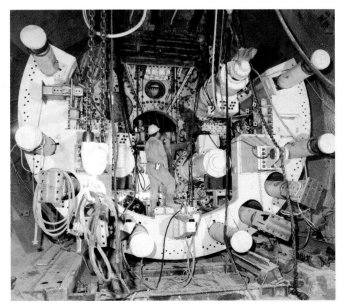

Assembling the UK landward service-tunnel TBM, which began its drive on 27 November.

By 1 December 1988 the cutterhead of the TBM for the northern undersea rail tunnel was nearing completion. It would take three months to assemble and commission the entire machine, which began its drive in late February 1989.

The paths of all three undersea tunnels from Shakespeare Cliff would cross the first attempt at a Channel tunnel, excavated with a Beaumont-English TBM a century before. The iron frames supporting the Beaumont tunnel had to be removed before the TBMs reached it. For safety reasons, this section of the old tunnel was filled with a low-strength grout.

Work was in progress on all three tunnels by late 1988 and quickly gathering pace.

By mid-December the southern landward rail-tunnel TBM, (T5), was being assembled at the foot of the Sangatte shaft. The white mechanism in the centre is the housing for the Archimedes screw, used to remove spoil from the head without permitting an inrush of water. T5 would begin its drive in mid-January, leaving the way clear to assemble the southern undersea rail-tunnel TBM, the last machine to start up on the French side.

After assembly at Dunkirk, the TBM for the northern undersea rail tunnel (T2) was lowered in sections into the Sangatte shaft. The weight of the complete machine, some 1,250 tonnes, far exceeded the capacity of the overhead gantry cranes.

12 August 1988: the T2 cutterhead seen in the marshalling area at the foot of the Sangatte shaft. Note the flat panels between the arms of the cutterhead. These would help to reduce the inflow of water when the TBM was driving through wet ground. The northern undersea rail tunnel drive began on 1 December.

In mid-August the back-up train of the undersea service-tunnel TBM at last cleared the bottom of the Sangatte shaft. After teething problems lasting several months, its performance began to improve during the autumn. By the end of the year it was advancing 60–70 m a week. Meanwhile T4, the second TBM to start up, was achieving 80–120 m a week in the landward service tunnel.

The workfaces needed a constant supply of materials from the pitheads.

Outbound trains on the narrow-gauge construction railways carried not only segment rings, but also grout, rails to extend the railway, pipes, electric cables, and so on.

Enormous quantities of concrete and special mortars were taken into the tunnels in a fleet of 'bullet' wagons. Pumps and pipes were then used to place the concrete exactly where it was needed.

Fresh air and emergency pumping facilities were essential to safe working practices.

As the tunnels lengthened, the ventilation from Sangatte and Shakespeare Cliff had to keep pace in order to ensure that there was fresh air throughout the system. Air was made to circulate through the tunnels by a system of fan stations and airlocks.

While tunnelling was in progress, there was always a small risk of water inrush from one of the unlined working faces. To counter this, emergency pump stations with very large capacity were installed at regular intervals. After the construction phase, permanent pump stations were built and the temporary stations removed. Once the final linings were in place, seepage into the tunnels proved to be far lower than anyone had predicted.

The operation made huge demands on power supplies and equipment.

As the TBMs moved forward, the electricity supply had continually to be extended. On each side of the Channel the demand for electricity in the tunnels was equivalent to the consumption of a sizeable town. On the UK side the peak was 23 megawatts, distributed through about 300 km of cable. The peak demand at Sangatte, recorded in November 1990, was 36 megawatts. This included the supply to the segment factory.

During the construction phase, the hot saline atmosphere could put machinery severely to the test. Equipment such as this bulldozer working far out under the Channel had to be maintained wherever it was.

Workshop staff fitting new teeth to a roadheader. Hundreds of people were employed on metalwork, carpentry, maintenance and repairs.

Two bridges were built across the Beussingue Trench. The nearer one in this photograph would carry the future A16 coastal motorway. The further bridge, which came into use in September 1988, was for the Route Nationale between Calais and Boulogne. While the bridges were being built, lorries carrying spoil to the terminal site bypassed them using a temporary construction road.

Two excavators capable of digging 1,000 cubic metres per hour had to remove nearly two million cubic metres of chalk in order to complete the Beussingue Trench. The trench is 800 m long and 30 m deep at the tunnel portal. Spoil was taken by lorry to areas of the terminal site where it could be used as fill.

On the French side, the removal of spoil from the Beussingue Trench was a major task in its own right.

Behind the railway fly-over works a drainage reservoir was taking shape. In the distance, the French terminal site had a strangely chequered appearance. In some parts the marshy subsoil had been covered with sand, elsewhere with chalk from the Beussingue Trench. Hidden underneath was a vast network of vertical and horizontal drains.

The railway flyover at the head of the Beussingue Trench would convert the future circuit taken by Eurotunnel's shuttle trains from a circle to a figure of eight.

In the future, shuttle trains would turn on a loop of track. For the moment, however, the path of the loop was marked only by the coating of sand laid to drain and consolidate the ground.

Earth-moving equipment gathered in the Beussingue Trench was testimony to the scale of the French terminal site. The construction work could be compared to building an international airport.

There were nearly a hundred plant species in Biggins Wood, 5 hectares of ancient woodland in the centre of the English terminal site. Before the area was cleared, smaller plants and seedlings were taken to Wye College for propagation. In September 1988 topsoil from the wood was moved to a new location on the northern boundary of the terminal. 'New Biggins Wood' has flourished. Monitoring shows that the great majority of species survived the move and are thriving in their new location.

The construction of the English terminal site posed different problems from the provision of sand fill to preservation of ancient woodland.

The site of the British terminal was, on average, 6 m below the required level. Rather than bringing in millions of tonnes of fill by road, 60,000 tonnes per week was delivered by pipeline. This material, dredged from the Goodwin Sands, was pumped to the site as a mixture of sand and seawater with the help of a very powerful pumping vessel. Between September 1988 and September 1989 some 2,600,000 cubic metres of sand were delivered to the terminal in this way.

From its station 800 m off Sandgate, the MV *Aquarius* pumped the mixture of sand and seawater at a speed of 4.5 m per second, to the terminal site 65 m above sea level and 4.2 km inland.

At the terminal site, the pipeline discharged the mixture of sand and seawater into artificial settling lagoons, from where the water was drained off and returned to the sea.

Machines called box scrapers were used to move sand and other fill around the site. Despite the well-known proverb, sand is an excellent fill material for this kind of civil engineering project.

By October 1988 the UK terminal, like its French counterpart, was chequered with earthworks made from different materials. One prominent feature in this view from the west was the path of the rail loop where the shuttle trains would turn. As it passes close to the villages of Newington and Peene, it would run in a tunnel. In addition, Eurotunnel undertook to buy any houses in these villages, up until 1997, at a market valuation which disregards their proximity to the terminal.

CHAPTER 6

January – June 1989

9 January:

Philippe Essig appointed full-time Chairman of TML.

16 January:

Start of French southern landward rail-tunnel drive (T5).

27 February:

Start of English northern undersea rail-tunnel drive.

26 March:

Start of southern French undersea rail-tunnel drive (T3).

27 April:

French landward service-tunnel drive (T4) completed.

9 May:

Jack Lemley appointed Chief Executive of TML.

10 June:

50,000th segment produced at Sangatte.

12 June:

Start of English southern undersea rail-tunnel drive.

On 10 February the English undersea service-tunnel drive reached 5 kilometres, one of the official milestones in the project, and morale was greatly improved. Internal reports began to speak with some confidence of a junction with the French service tunnel before the end of 1990. Overall, 8 kilometres was bored in the first

schedule. In the final stages, the TBM had been slowed down in order to delay the breakthrough until the date set for the ceremony.

However, not all the news was good. Tenders for building the shuttle locomotives and wagons were much higher than forecast. One reason for this

> *Overall, 8 kilometres was bored in the first quarter of 1989 compared to 5 in the second half of 1988.*

quarter of 1989 compared to 5 in the second half of 1988. By June, TML had a very strong team of senior managers led by Jack Lemley, an American engineer with long experience of major projects.

The first breakthroughs, at Castle Hill and the French portal, also made welcome news. Despite poor geological conditions the French landward service-tunnel drive was completed two months ahead of

was that the rolling-stock industry was enjoying a glut of orders. The likely cost increase would more than outweigh any reductions that might be achieved elsewhere. Moreover, it was clear by the end of June that there would be cost overruns in several other areas as well.

Improved tunnelling progress on the English side was marred by a fatal accident in January and a second in February.

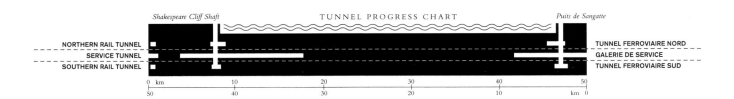

Shakespeare Cliff Shaft — TUNNEL PROGRESS CHART — *Puits de Sangatte*

NORTHERN RAIL TUNNEL — TUNNEL FERROVIAIRE NORD
SERVICE TUNNEL — GALERIE DE SERVICE
SOUTHERN RAIL TUNNEL — TUNNEL FERROVIAIRE SUD

March 1989: a typical scene at the Lower Shakespeare Cliff pithead, where a series of overhead gantry cranes transferred segments *(centre left)*, arriving in rail wagons from the Isle of Grain to stockpiles; and from the stockpiles to construction trains *(centre right)*.

The TBM for the northern undersea rail tunnel was assembled during the first two months of the year, and the drive began on 27 February. By June it had reached the wet fragmented ground encountered earlier by the service-tunnel drive. The difficult conditions, which lasted for about 2.7 km, caused several weeks' delay to all three British undersea TBMs, since they had been designed to work in dry rock. Necessary modifications included a trailing hood at the rear of the TBM, sheltering the area where the lining rings were built. This prevented loose material falling from the tunnel roof.

On 5 April the cutterhead frame of the northern landward rail-tunnel TBM was lowered in one piece down the ventilation shaft at Shakespeare Cliff. The white cladding just behind the cutter-head was to protect an Alimak personnel lift which ran down the side of the shaft. Only one TBM had yet to be delivered on the British side: the machine for the southern landward rail tunnel. At this date it was still undergoing factory tests.

In early 1989 the TBMs for the undersea rail tunnels were assembled in situ.

By 29 March the southern undersea rail-tunnel cutterhead had been moved forward into a section of tunnel excavated in advance, known as the thrust chamber. The move made space in the main chamber to assemble the back-up train. The drive began on 12 June.

The southern undersea rail-tunnel TBM was lowered in pieces down the ventilation shaft and assembly began on 7 February. This photograph, taken on 27 February, shows work in progress at the rear of the cutterhead.

For environmental reasons the English landward tunnels were extended under Holywell in 'cut and cover' tunnels.

The landward tunnels bored by TBMs from Lower Shakespeare Cliff could have emerged in this valley, known as Holywell, which is immediately to the east of the terminal site. However, it was argued on environmental grounds that the rail tracks across Holywell should be covered over.

This view looking east, taken in June 1989, shows the walls of the rail tunnels largely in place with a partial cross-over built between them. The other half of the cross-over would be just inside the UK portal.

Above: TBMs could not operate close to the surface, so their drives stopped at the eastern edge of Holywell. The rail tracks would cross the valley hidden in 'cut and cover' tunnels. For this, the first step was to dig a deep trench, seen here in October 1988.

The tunnels at this point were approaching the British portal. As shown in this photograph looking west, at Holywell the service tunnel dipped down to pass below the southern rail tunnel. It would emerge at the portal on one side of the rail tunnels rather than between them.

On 17 April the service tunnel under Castle Hill broke through into the unfinished structure of the British portal at the eastern end of the terminal site. The sign reads 'Paris 325 km, next services 65 km'. This was the first of 14 breakthroughs during the construction of the Channel Tunnel.

Between Holywell and the terminal site stands Castle Hill. The three tunnels were driven through it using roadheaders.

The British portal was built using the 'top down' method. First, the tunnel walls were created by sinking reinforced-concrete piles side-by-side. Then the roof slab was poured. Finally, as shown (above), the tunnel itself was excavated by removing the earth beneath the roof slab.

The New Austrian Tunnelling Method (NATM) was used for the primary linings in the Castle Hill tunnels

A passing bay in the service tunnel under Castle Hill, seen here in December 1988 before the final concrete lining was cast.

On 27 April T4, the French landward service-tunnel TBM, broke through into the Beussingue Trench.

The event was witnessed by a crowd of VIPs, journalists, photographers and TV crews. On either side of the portal stood giant portraits of King François I of France and King Henry VIII of England. In 1520 the two monarchs met near Calais in such splendour that their encampment was dubbed the Field of the Cloth of Gold.

Emerging through the cutterhead, the crew celebrated their success. The Marubeni-Mitsubishi machine had taken nine months to drive the 3.2 km from Sangatte. In March it had set a new world record for a closed-mode TBM: 886 m.

Its task completed T4 was taken back to Sangatte by road and put up for sale.

*By the summer of 1989
the spoil-transport system
at Lower Shakespeare Cliff
was in full swing.*

Wagons full of chalk arriving from the TBMs had special bodies which tilted sideways, dumping the spoil onto conveyors that ran in tunnels underneath the tracks.

The underground conveyor systems for each tunnel took the spoil to Adit A1, where a further conveyor brought it to the surface. Equipment of this kind was readily available, since it has long been used in the mining industry.

Still more conveyors moved the spoil across the pithead site to a large stockpile. Here it was loaded into trucks for its final journey to one of the artificial lagoons inside the new sea walls at the foot of the cliff.

At the foot of the Sangatte shaft, construction trains ran through one of three 'tipplers'. Those in line with the rail tunnels were double, with a capacity of six wagons at a time, while the third, in line with the service tunnel, could handle three wagons. Special couplings allowed the tipplers to upturn part of a spoil train without affecting the wagons on either side.

Spoil from the upturned wagons was funnelled into crushers, where any large lumps of chalk were broken up.

Fifteen metres below the tipplers water was added to the crushed chalk in one of five large mixing vats. Heavy chains suspended from rotating arms stirred the mixture until it resembled yoghurt. The slurry was then allowed to flow down through traps to the pumps in the lowest level of the shaft.

In the lower regions of the Sangatte shaft, rarely seen by visitors, technicians watched over every stage of the spoil treatment.

The pump room of the Sangatte shaft was 68 m below sea level. Eight massive pumps sent slurry from the mixing vats up pipes leading to Fond Pignon.
Water removed from the tunnels was stored in reservoirs at the side of the shaft and used in the mixing vats. Any surplus went for treatment at the surface, propelled on its way by four pumps with a combined capacity of 1,400 litres per second.

The slurry pipes from Sangatte to Fond Pignon were 1,500–1,800 m long, and climbed 130 m from the pumps at the base of the shaft.

At the end of each slurry pipe, the spoil poured into an ever-growing lake of chalk behind the Fond Pignon dam. By the time the tunnels were completed, the two blockhouses seen here had disappeared under the surface of the lake.

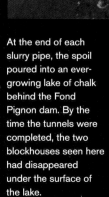

Above: By late June 1989 preparations were in hand to raise the embankment at Fond Pignon. The new dam, in places 30 m high, would now be 990 m long. Behind it the capacity of the lake would be more than doubled to 3.3 million cubic metres.

In May 1989 the site of the French rail-tunnel portal was clearly visible at the lower end of the Beussingue Trench. As in England, the service tunnel had been moved to one side from its normal position between the rail tunnels before it reached the portal. The landward-drive TBM can be seen here at its entrance. Just below the TBM, work was in progress building a pumping station which would keep the Beussingue Trench free of water.

Below: In the spring of 1989, the earthworks can now be seen to extend from the Beussingue Trench in the foreground to the rail loop far beyond. At the western limit of the terminal, a line of roadworks *(left)* marks the path of the future coastal motorway.

Above: Most road vehicles entering and leaving the French terminal would do so through a circular interchange on the coastal motorway, whose route runs across this photograph. In the foreground *(lower left)* is Fort Nieulay, an 18th-century Vauban fort from which the interchange would take its name. The pattern of the roadworks was confused at this stage by a temporary construction road, seen here running from top to bottom of the picture.

The first sand was pumped to the English terminal site in September 1988. By the following spring the results were spectacular. Before the pipeline was shut down in September 1989 it had saved around half a million lorry movements.

As originally conceived, the terminal would have drained towards its western end, where a stream provided a natural outflow to the sea. Concerns about possible damage to local ecology led to a radical change of plan. The site was redesigned to drain towards the eastern end where a new relief sewer 1.8 m in diameter was bored to the sea.

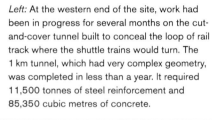

Left: At the western end of the site, work had been in progress for several months on the cut-and-cover tunnel built to conceal the loop of rail track where the shuttle trains would turn. The 1 km tunnel, which had very complex geometry, was completed in less than a year. It required 11,500 tonnes of steel reinforcement and 85,350 cubic metres of concrete.

The terminals serve as an interchange between the tunnel system and the national road and rail networks. In the UK a link known as the Continental Main Line was built from the tunnel portal to existing British Rail track west of the terminal site. In order to reach this track, the new line had to cross the A20 and the new M20 motorway at the western end of the terminal. This meant building a five-span bridge 175 m long which would, in due course, carry a heavier load than any other public bridge in Britain.

CHAPTER 7

July – December 1989

26 July:

Orders for Eurotunnel's shuttle-service rolling stock announced.

1 August:

English undersea service-tunnel drive reaches 10 km.

2 August:

Start of English northern landward rail-tunnel drive.

August:

Peter Allwood appointed TML UK Construction Director.

3 October:

French undersea service-tunnel drive reaches 5 km.

9 November:

English landward service-tunnel drive completed.

27 November:

Start of English southern landward rail-tunnel drive.

18 December:

French southern landward rail-tunnel drive (T5) completed.

19 December:

British Rail and SNCF order 30 high-speed train-sets from a consortium led by GEC and Alsthom.

On 21 July, following a Eurotunnel board meeting in Paris, it was announced that the high cost of shuttle rolling stock together with other cost increases meant that additional funding would be required over and above the debt facilities and equity already in place.

A few days later the rolling-stock orders were announced. The cost of 40 electric locomotives, 252 HGV (heavy goods vehicle) wagons and 252 wagons for cars, coaches and motorcycles totalled £600 million, compared to an original estimate of £226 million.

During the autumn, lengthy negotiations took place between Eurotunnel, TML, and the banking syndicate over costs and financing. These talks attracted a huge amount of press speculation, much of it very negative in tone.

Press foreboding should have been tempered by the encouraging rates of progress in most of the tunnels. Only the TBMs in the English undersea railtunnels were performing badly, slowed by the early stretch of bad ground, but the service-tunnel drive had shown that

> *All three of the French undersea drives were ahead of target. By the end of the year the service-tunnel machines were approaching one another at 380 m a week.*

conditions there would soon improve. All three of the French undersea drives were ahead of target. By the end of the year the service-tunnel machines were approaching one another at 380 m a week.

In November, British Rail announced a partnership with a private consortium called Eurorail to build the high-speed link. Eurotunnel welcomed the news.

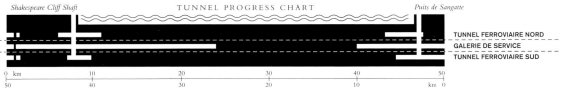

Shakespeare Cliff Shaft — TUNNEL PROGRESS CHART — *Puits de Sangatte*

NORTHERN RAIL TUNNEL / TUNNEL FERROVIAIRE NORD
SERVICE TUNNEL / GALERIE DE SERVICE
SOUTHERN RAIL TUNNEL / TUNNEL FERROVIAIRE SUD

0 km 10 20 30 40 50
50 40 30 20 10 km 0

Mid-October 1989: the sea walls enclosing the western spoil lagoon at the Shakespeare Cliff site would soon meet. As the spoil added land to the platform, the site facilities improved. The new buildings erected included workshops and stores, as well as a repair shop for the construction railway. During the summer, when the persistent drought brought water shortages, a desalination plant was installed so that fresh water could be obtained from the sea.

Conditions underground in the English undersea rail drives made autumn 1989 a testing time.

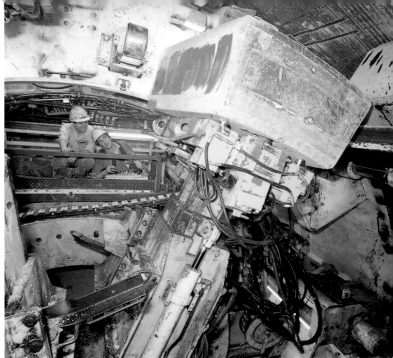

On 8 August work began on the assembly of the final TBM on the English side. The southern landward rail-tunnel drive began on 27 November. The photograph *(above)* of one of the last factory tests gives an unusual view of segments being placed in the build area. The ring of red girders represents the wall of the tunnel.

During the autumn the English undersea rail drives were bedevilled by wet and fragmented ground. Both TBMs were stopped for modifications. For example, the upper segment conveyors were removed, making more space available for grouting. These changes led to some improvement but, as with the service tunnel, the difficulties would continue until the drives reached dry rock.

Meanwhile, work on the rail tunnels beneath the Holywell site was nearing completion.

This photograph taken in August 1989 shows the relationship between the Holywell tunnels in the foreground and the terminal site beyond Castle Hill. By the end of the year the Holywell tunnels were almost complete. Early in 1990 the site would be handed over to contractors building an extension of the M20/A20 dual carriageway. This would skirt round the base of Castle Hill, passing above the rail tunnels before entering two road tunnels through the hillside on the right.

The shotcrete NATM primary lining in the rail tunnels under Castle Hill looked like an illustration from a Victorian fairy tale, but not for long. As soon as the tunnels had broken through, work began on the inner concrete linings.

Above: The northern rail-tunnel break-through under Castle Hill, seen from inside the tunnel, took place on 14 September. This was the last of the short tunnels between Holywell and the terminal to be completed.

Above: On 9 August the southern rail tunnel under Castle Hill broke through into the portal structure at the terminal. The roadheader is seen here from the portal, cutting away the final wall of rock.

On 9 November 1989 the landward service-tunnel TBM broke through into a reception chamber prepared for it at the eastern edge of Holywell. This was the first TBM breakthrough on the British side and, like its French predecessor, it attracted worldwide publicity. The drive had averaged 175 m a week during the 8 km journey from Shakespeare Cliff, reaching its destination a fortnight ahead of schedule. At breakthrough the TBM was just 4 mm off a 'perfect' centreline, a degree of accuracy which augured well for the meeting of the undersea drives.

By the end of the year, much of the permanent concrete lining had been placed in the Castle Hill tunnels. First, the NATM primary lining was covered with a waterproof membrane, then the inner lining was cast. This photograph shows a lined section of the service tunnel.

By November 1989 the portal structure at the British terminal had been completely excavated and the floor was being laid. The walls, formed by bored concrete piling before excavation began, would shortly be given an inner lining. There is space inside the portal structure for a cross-over between the two tunnel rail tracks, twin to the cross-over under Holywell.

Each day, the progress of the TBMs was posted on a board above the personnel lifts in the Sangatte shaft. This encouraged a lively spirit of competition between the crews. On 14 August 1989 most of the drives on the French side were ahead of programme. By the end of the year the figures would be still more impressive.

		BRIGITTE		EUROPA		CATHERINE		PASCALINE	
TERRE	MER	REALISE m/l	OBJECTIF MINIMUM	REALISE m/l	OBJECTIF MINIMUM	REALISE m/l	OBJECTIF MINIMUM	REALISE m/l	OBJECTIF MINIMUM
PUITS		0,0	16,3	17,6	10,0	9,6	5,5	12,7	12,0
AVANCEMENT DU 13		92,4	211,9	118,4	130,0	27,2	71,5	191,8	156,0
AVANCEMENT DEPUIS LE 1er		550,1	498,0	434,3	279,0	180,9	78,0	110,4	0,0
OBJECTIF MINIMUM									
PM DU TUNNELIER		4047,1	39329	17005	15150	7695	4680	8410	9930

During the summer the construction railway was still running through the completed service tunnel between Sangatte and the Beussingue Trench. In October, however, the tracks were removed so that work could begin laying the permanent concrete floor.

The control cabin of T3, which drove 1,470 m of the southern undersea rail tunnel during the last quarter of 1989. This was almost three times its rate of progress six months earlier.

While the landward TBMs had been built to an established design, these undersea machines incorporated new technology. Notably, they were able to withstand water pressures of 10 bar. Experience gained during the start-up period led to modifications, and the cutterheads of the rail-tunnel TBMs had now been strengthened.

The main structure of the Beussingue portal was built during the autumn, in time for the T5 breakthrough in mid-December.

On 18 December the northern rail tunnel reached the Beussingue Trench. Despite a five-week halt, T5 was a fortnight ahead of its schedule. It had bored 3.2 km in ten months. The crews celebrated the breakthrough with Pierre Matheron *(in a dark coat, centre right)* and Jacques Fermin *(extreme left)*, TML's senior construction managers on the French side.

In the summer of 1989 the French terminal still resembled patchwork, but the earthworks, which totalled 11 million cubic metres, would be practically finished by the end of the year. In this view looking north-east towards Calais, the future platform area can be seen to the left of the central construction road. Three curved ramps mark the start of work on the platform overbridges.

The lining of the reservoirs is a synthetic waterproof material, laid in strips which are joined together to form a continuous membrane.

During the autumn, earthworks for the shuttle loop track continued. The structure in the foreground is one of the terminal's five drainage reservoirs, each walled-in by raised dykes so that it stands above ground level. These reservoirs are fed by six pump stations linked to 10 km of canals, and their combined capacity is nearly 300,000 cubic metres. Work on the canal feeding this reservoir can be seen to its left.

In the autumn of 1989 pillars were cast for the first of the four bridges which would span the shuttle platforms. Three rows of pillars were needed for a deck up to 20 m wide. Today, this first overbridge is the exit bridge for vehicles disembarking from the front of shuttle trains.

By mid-December many of the deck beams were in place. The construction was well ahead of other works in the platform area, where ground consolidation was still in progress.

On 9 December the last concrete was poured on the roof of the loop tunnel. Soon, this vast structure would be buried under landscaped earthworks, built up high to screen the noise and activity of the terminal from neighbouring villages.

As the tunnels approaching the terminals neared completion the access bridges were taking shape.

By August 1989 the access routes at the western end of the terminal could clearly be seen. The road bridges on the right would become the access and exit routes for traffic using the westbound M20 leading to London and beyond. The wider bridges on the left would carry the Continental Main Line. This would join existing British Rail track at Dollands Moor, the cleared land visible in the distance to the left of the motorway. The road in the foreground, yet to be bridged, is the A20.

Right: The access bridges shown above are in the top left-hand corner of this view of the western end of the terminal taken in mid-October. Two features which stand out are the line of the loop tunnel, now nearly completed, and the earthworks for the Continental Main Line running up the centre of the terminal towards Dollands Moor.

At the English terminal, as in France, work on the first platform overbridge began during the autumn. There are differences in the regulations for railway bridges in the two countries and these led to radically different designs. The English bridges rest on massive piers in the form of a box with reinforced-concrete sides. This dawn photograph shows the first of these boxes under construction.

On both sides of the Channel there were different designs of manrider. All of them were diesel-powered.

Lower Shakespeare Cliff: segments, equipment and all other materials going in or out of the English tunnels used one of the five rack-and-pinion tracks in Adit A2.

There were rail tracks in the goods lift at the Sangatte Shaft, making it possible to move emergency equipment and other rolling stock between the tunnels and the surface.

Electric locomotives recharged their batteries in the marshalling area at Shakespeare Cliff so that they could run in areas where there was no catenary. There were similar provisions in France.

Both Shakespeare Cliff and Sangatte remained the centre of busy logistical networks feeding the tunnelling operations.

At the entrance to each tunnel in the Sangatte shaft was a marshalling area linked by cross-passages to its neighbours. These links gave added flexibility to the railway system.

In the French tunnels the semi-liquid spoil splashed onto trains and tracks creating a potential hazard. Here spoil wagons in the northern rail tunnel are hosed down as they pass through the air-lock at Sangatte.

There was hardly any surplus space in the service tunnel, seen here on the English side. Tunnel works of any kind meant closing one track for several hundred metres. There were strict safety rules for both trains and personnel.

*Operations had to be
closely monitored by the control
centre at all times.*

The main control room
for the English tunnels
at Shakespeare Cliff
worked day and night.
It received data from
monitoring equipment
throughout the tun-
nels. In addition, each
tunnel had its own
railway control board
which often managed
fifteen trains at a time.

Driving a locomotive in Adit A1, the first stretch of
track in the English construction railway to be laid
and the last to be dismantled. Drivers kept in
touch with the control centre by radio.

Above: The whole of
the French construction
railway was displayed on
a mimic panel in the con-
trol centre above the
Sangatte shaft. All the
other systems in the
tunnels were controlled
from this room.

Left: The marine control
station at the foot of Adit A2.

The Channel Tunnel
construction railway
was the third largest
railway network in
Britain after British
Rail and London
Underground. Work-
shops on Lower
Shakespeare Cliff
maintained 135
locomotives and 900
purpose-built wagons.

The French construc-
tion railway was hardly
less impressive. In May
1991 the fleet in daily
use totalled 700 units.
On both sides of the
Channel the rolling
stock was modified in
TML's workshops to
overcome problems
and meet the changing

January – June 1990

On 7 January the total of tunnel bored reached 50 km. Two days later Eurotunnel and TML reached an agreement on costs. This was incorporated in an amendment to the construction contract signed on 20 February.

Tunnelling progress, so long a matter for concern, was now very good indeed, even in the English undersea rail tunnels.

was no legal basis for a truly binational company. In this respect, as in many others, the lawyers who helped set up the project had to find solutions to completely unprecedented legal problems.

The successful continuation of the project was marred during this period by further fatal accidents, particularly on the English side where Jack Lemley and Peter

Tunnelling progress, so long a matter for concern, was now very good indeed.

By the middle of the year all anxiety on that score had ceased.

In late January André Bénard was named Chairman of the Joint Anglo-French Eurotunnel Board while Alastair Morton became deputy Chairman and Chief Executive, a post he would hold until after the TML handover in December 1993. The Joint Board unites the legal structures of Eurotunnel PLC and Eurotunnel SA, two national companies which operate, to all intents and purposes, as a single unit.

When Eurotunnel was formed there

Allwood began a crusade for greater safety. While many commentators pointed out that the number of accidents was not exceptional for underground work, TML management rejected any idea that there was an 'acceptable' level of serious injuries. This philosophy gradually bore fruit.

In early June the British government confirmed that it was unwilling to contribute public funds to a high-speed rail link. This decision, generally attributed to Margaret Thatcher, was greeted with almost universal condemnation. It brought the Eurorail project to a halt.

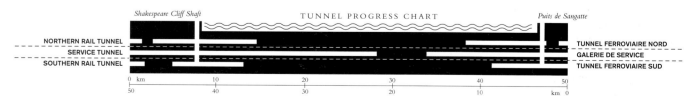

Shakespeare Cliff Shaft — TUNNEL PROGRESS CHART — *Puits de Sangatte*

NORTHERN RAIL TUNNEL / TUNNEL FERROVIAIRE NORD
SERVICE TUNNEL / GALERIE DE SERVICE
SOUTHERN RAIL TUNNEL / TUNNEL FERROVIAIRE SUD

This simple but effective way to store clothing
was adopted from the mining industry. Working
and personal clothes alternate on hooks raised to
the ceiling by individual locking pulley systems.
The suspended garments are dried by warm air.
This 'hangman's hall' at Shakespeare Cliff
duplicated the 'salle des pendus' at Sangatte.

*As the land platform at
Shakespeare Cliff grew larger
more spoil lagoons were built.*

The sea wall enclosing the western spoil lagoon
was completed on 6 April. This was the last of
the spoil lagoons originally planned.
In all, 134,000 cubic metres of concrete had
been used to build the 1,400 m sea wall, and
the lagoons were one of the largest sheet-piling
projects in the world. In June work started on a
new lagoon at the eastern end of the platform.
This would hold spoil previously intended for
use as fill on the terminal site.

The growing land platform at Lower Shakespeare
Cliff made it necessary to lengthen the spoil
conveyor. A radial spreader *(bottom)* mounted on
caterpillar tracks was commissioned in March.
Additional space was used to enlarge the segment stockpile and prepare for installing fixed
equipment in the tunnels.

Conditions in the worst section of wet ground were significantly improved by injecting silica grout from the service tunnel into the path of the rail-tunnel TBMs. The effect was to fill and seal water-bearing fissures. The technique had also been used during the early part of the French undersea drives.

Despite continuing wet ground during the first months of the year, the modified undersea rail-tunnel TBMs were now making better progress. By the summer, conditions were much improved and in June the northern rail-tunnel machine set a new world record for a TBM of its type by driving 329 m in a week.

At two points under the English Channel the rail tunnels come together so that trains can cross from one tunnel into the other. The cross-overs, normally closed off by steel doors, will be used in the early hours of the morning to make sections of Tunnel available for maintenance. They could also make it easier to evacuate trains from the Tunnel in an emergency.

The cross-over on the English side was built before the rail-tunnel TBMs had reached the site. It was therefore excavated from the service tunnel, which had been driven downwards and to the north at this point in order to be well clear of the workings. In August 1989 a Voest-Alpine roadheader started driving access tunnels from the service tunnel to the cross-over site. A second roadheader arrived in October. By the end of March 1990 two parallel arched side drifts had been cut and lined with shotcrete NATM reinforcement. After this, work began excavating the crown of the cavern across the top of the two side drifts. Much of this had been completed by the end of June. The last stage of the excavation would be to cut away the inner side-drift linings and the bench of rock between them.

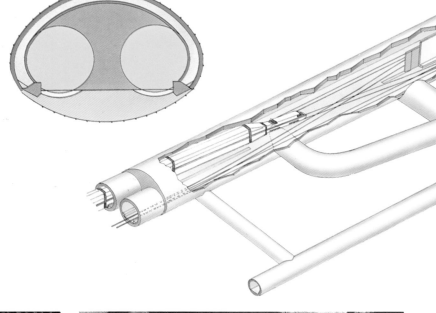

In July 1989, before the first roadheader arrived, hand tunnellers excavated rooms to house a temporary electrical substation and a compressor station.

The UK cross-over was excavated by roadheaders, starting from the service tunnel.

In November 1989 the huge Voest-Alpine roadheaders began excavating the side drifts.

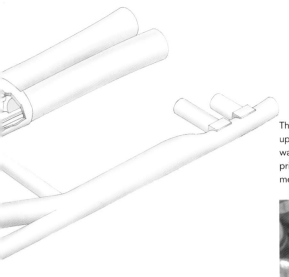

The more vertical of the side-drift walls, leading up to the point of the arch, would be part of the wall of the finished cavern. Here, the NATM primary lining was heavily reinforced with steel mesh and rockbolts or dowells up to 8 m long.

During this work enormous amounts of spoil and materials had to pass through the service tunnel in addition to the construction trains required for the service-tunnel TBM. The crane operator *(right)* was stationed at the junction of the service tunnel and the main access tunnel sloping up to the cross-over workings.

By May work was well advanced excavating the crown of the cross-over cavern above the two side drifts.

Holywell and Castle Hill nearing completion.

By February 1990 the cut-and-cover tunnels across Holywell were about to disappear. The large round holes in the foreground gave access to two of the TBM dismantling chambers at the ends of the landward drives from Shakespeare Cliff.

On 8 January 1990 the TBM that had driven the northern landward rail tunnel (T5) made a spectacular about-turn in front of the French portal. Supported on air cushions, it was repositioned at the portal to the southern rail tunnel. After maintenance and repairs, and with its back-up train in place, it would drive back to Sangatte. It was the only Channel-Tunnel TBM to be used twice.

During the spring, work continued casting the final concrete linings in the rail tunnels under Castle Hill. This view in the northern tunnel shows the waterproof membrane fixed in position ready for casting to begin.

T5, the northern landward rail-tunnel

TBM, was turned at the French portal to be

redeployed on the southern rail-tunnel.

On the French side undersea tunnelling was progressing well ahead of the schedule.

In the first half of 1990 the TBMs produced remarkable results. An incessant round of construction trains, directed from a central control room at Sangatte, kept up with their need for segments and materials and carried off their spoil. The TBMs went faster still. In the second quarter, the speed of the undersea service tunnel passed 1,200 m a month. By the end of June all three undersea drives were way ahead of programme: by 12 weeks in the service tunnel, by 17 and 23 weeks in the rail tunnels. Even in difficult ground, there were no major delays. Meanwhile, in the bowels of the Sangatte shaft, spoil treatment was being perfected.

The Sangatte pithead during the height of its activity. In the foreground, the section of tunnel marked Eurotunnel's French Exhibition Centre, opened in 1987. It received hundreds of thousands of visitors a year.

For its return journey to Sangatte, T5 became T6. The start of the drive was celebrated on 5 March at a ceremony in the Beussingue Trench when Pierre Matheron, TML's Construction Director, France, was formally invested as a Chevalier de la Légion d'Honneur. He is seen here *(right)* with one of his grandchildren and Philippe Essig, Chairman of TML.

A tippler empties spoil from a construction train serving T6. As the drive was working towards Sangatte, it was easier to place the spoil into a pit on the terminal than transport it to the shaft.

After the T6 back-up train had disappeared on its way back to Sangatte, the portal at the lower end of the Beussingue Trench began to take on its final appearance. Note, however, the ventilation fan and ducting leading to T6 in the right-hand tunnel.

As the working face moved further from the coast, journeys by construction train at each end of the shift became longer and longer.

Sangatte shaft: the marshalling area at the entrance to the undersea service tunnel.

At both ends of the tunnel there were systems to identify those working underground. This precaution, essential in the event of an emergency, assumed new significance once the tunnel entrances had become an international frontier. TML's full-height turnstiles on the British side reflected the concerns of the British Customs and Immigration authorities.

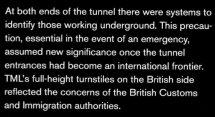

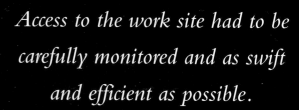

Access to the work site had to be carefully monitored and as swift and efficient as possible.

At Shakespeare Cliff as at Sangatte, the workforce used lifts for access to the tunnel system.

TBM crews, each numbering from 20 to 50 people, were only part of the huge underground workforce on each side of the Channel.
As the tunnel system extended, the construction railways had to provide regular passenger services for journeys which could take one and a half hours or more each way.

Tunnel workings under the Channel may seem a bleak spot for a tea-break, but the working temperature was often tropical and there was plenty of good humour. Visitors to the French workings were sometimes surprised to come upon little cabins which could look strangely out of place in such surroundings.

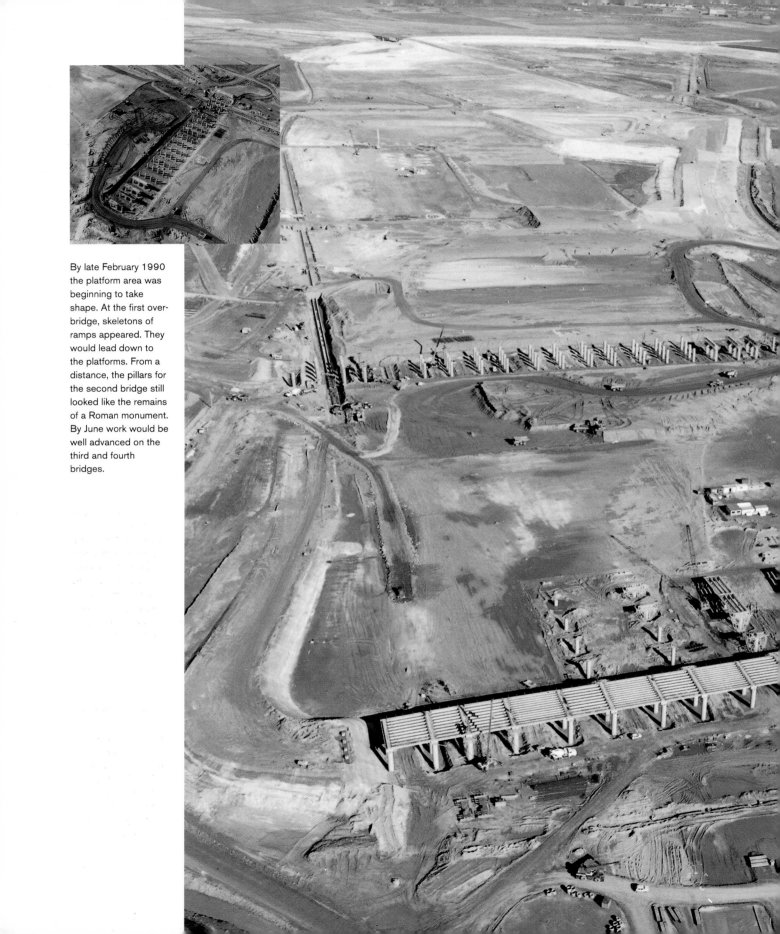

By late February 1990 the platform area was beginning to take shape. At the first over-bridge, skeletons of ramps appeared. They would lead down to the platforms. From a distance, the pillars for the second bridge still looked like the remains of a Roman monument. By June work would be well advanced on the third and fourth bridges.

At the French terminal, bridge construction progressed hand in hand with other work on the platform site.

The first step in the bridge construction was to bore holes for concrete foundation piles under each pillar, reaching down to solid chalk.

The timing of different works in the platform area was determined by the state of consolidation of the ground beneath. In this photograph taken in April 1990 part of the heavy surcharge of sand is being removed.

A transverse footing was poured across the width of the bridge, linking the piles under all three pillars. Then the pillars themselves, 1.8 m in diameter, were cast inside cylindrical steel shuttering.

May 1990: excavating a drainage canal beside the shuttle loop. The French terminal has systems to cope with two quite separate sources of water. First, there is ground water, whose level is unaffected by seasons or the weather. It has to be pumped constantly to keep the level beneath the surface in low-lying areas of the terminal and the Beussingue Trench. Second, surface and waste water has to be drained and treated where appropriate. A water-treatment plant built for the latter purpose also serves the neighbouring community of Coquelles.

Late-February 1990: casting reinforced-concrete piers for Overbridge One.

Late-April 1990: the ramps and piers of Overbridge One and the start of work on Overbridge Two.

The massive overbridges soon became the most prominent feature of the English terminal.

During the first half of 1990 there was progress on earthworks, retaining walls, drainage and other projects on various parts of the site. The most visible construction, however, was work on three of the four platform overbridges. From now on, these massive structures would dominate the terminal.

May 1990: beginning the decking of Overbridge One. In the background, the portal of the loop tunnel.

CHAPTER 9

July – December 1990

13 August:

Total of tunnel drives reaches 100 km.

11 September:

English northern landward rail-tunnel drive completed.

25 October:

Eurotunnel signs agreements for £1.8 billion additional bank credit facilities.

30 October:

First contact between the French and English undersea service-tunnel drives.

31 October:

French service-tunnel drive (T1) completed.

3 November:

English undersea service-tunnel drive completed.

20 November:

English southern landward rail-tunnel drive completed.

29 November:

French northern landward rail-tunnel drive (T6) completed.

1 December:

Undersea service tunnel breakthrough linking English and French workings.

3 December:

Eurotunnel rights issue completed, raising a further £566 million.

21 December 1988:

Christmas lights on the terminal at the end of a remarkable year.

The second half of 1990 was, in many ways, the most remarkable period in the construction of the tunnel. The TBMs were achieving record progress, and their advance placed ever-greater demands on the construction railway. Tens of thousands of tonnes of segments and spoil were moved every day. Work in the service-tunnel drives, particularly on the English side where the face was more than 10 km in advance of the rail tunnels, posed exceptional problems of ventilation and safety. The equipment used to monitor conditions was alleged to be so sensitive that if someone lit a cigarette in a cross-passage the control room would soon detect it.

In August Eurotunnel announced that the corporate headquarters would remain in London, while the operating headquarters of the future transport system would be housed in a new building at the French terminal.

The first contact between the two undersea service-tunnel drives gave rise to much comment in the press about the end

> ## *The first contact between the two undersea service-tunnel drives gave rise to much comment in the press about the end of England's status as an island.*

of England's status as an island. The future of Britain's relationship with Europe was a burning issue at the time, linked to a government leadership crisis. By 1 December, when a doorway between the two tunnels was hacked out by Graham Fagg and Philippe Cozette, Margaret Thatcher was no longer the British premier.

Before the end of 1990 Eurotunnel had secured additional bank funding and completed a rights issue. The project was set to continue.

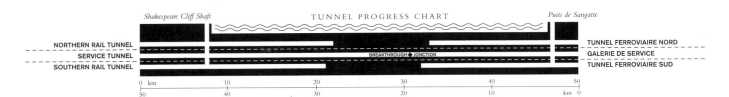

Shakespeare Cliff Shaft — TUNNEL PROGRESS CHART — Puits de Sangatte

NORTHERN RAIL TUNNEL — TUNNEL FERROVIAIRE NORD
SERVICE TUNNEL — BREAKTHROUGH ◆ JONCTION — GALERIE DE SERVICE
SOUTHERN RAIL TUNNEL — TUNNEL FERROVIAIRE SUD

0 km ... 10 ... 20 ... 30 ... 40 ... 50
50 ... 40 ... 30 ... 20 ... 10 ... km 0

The Lower Shakespeare Cliff site, brilliantly lit in
early December. Work here, as in the tunnels,
continued round the clock. The final spoil lagoon
was nearing completion, and a second desalination plant had been built because local water
supplies could not meet the demand.

On 11 September the northern landward rail-tunnel TBM broke through into its reception chamber at Holywell. It had climbed 86 m from its starting-point under Shakespeare Cliff. Four shifts totalling 144 men had crewed the machine, which was an early record-breaker. In the last few hundred metres, wet and fragmented rock had made conditions extremely difficult.

The ground ahead of the TBM had been treated by injecting grout from the service tunnel at pressures of up to 18 bars.

On 8 November the thousandth segment train from the Isle of Grain arrived at Shakespeare Cliff. By this time the precast works had produced some 400,000 segments. Now, as tunnels were completed, production was slowing down.

By November, the English portal at the eastern end of the terminal was almost complete.

The UK cross-over, 17 km from the English portal, is probably the largest cavern ever built under the sea. By the beginning of August the northern rail-tunnel TBM was waiting to pass through, so work continued night and day to remove the inner walls of the side drifts and the remaining rock between them.

The UK cross-over, a vast submarine cavern, was constructed ahead of the rail tunnels.

'Eyes' were prepared at each end of the cross-over cavern where the rail-tunnel TBMs would break through.

On 27 August the northern rail-tunnel TBM entered the cross-over. It was just 35 mm off the perfect centreline.

One of the road-headers which excavated the cross-over is dwarfed by northern rail-tunnel TBM, 265 m long and weighing 1350 tonnes. The drive recommenced at the far end of the cross-over on 7 September.

An unusual view into the area where the segment rings were built. The TBMs propelled themselves through the cross-over on temporary rails, laying a line of lower segments for their hydraulic jacks to push against.

The southern rail-tunnel TBM entered the cross-over on 19 September and resumed its drive at the far end on 28 September. As excavated, the cavern was 163.8 m long, 21.2 m wide, and 15.4 m high. The massive inner concrete lining, built after the TBMs had passed through, would reduce the internal dimensions to 156 m long, 18.1 m wide, and 9.5 m high (track-level to crown). The two red cables in the foreground, left, were the 11.5 kilovolt ring-main power supply for the northern rail-tunnel TBM.

The southern rail-tunnel TBM
penetrated the cross-over cavern then,
nine days later, resumed its journey
on the other side.

On 20 November the northern landward rail-tunnel drive reached Holywell. All three landward tunnels from Shakespeare Cliff now ran through to the terminal. The TBM, the last to set out, had broken at least four world records for a machine of its type. In June 1990 it had driven 1,222 m.

Nine days later the French landward tunnels were completed when the rail-tunnel TBM which had started out from Sangatte in January 1989 returned to the shaft.

By late 1990 all the landward rail tunnels in both France and England had been completed.

By the summer of 1990 Fond Pignon was once again almost full. In part, this was the price paid for the success of the French undersea TBMs, which had bored more tunnel than originally planned. Another reason, however, was that the spoil mix from Sangatte was fine and extremely fluid. The surface of Fond Pignon therefore tended to level out to the edge of the dam, whereas the aim had been to create a slope.

In three and a half months' work, more than 250,000 tonnes of earth were added, raising the dam to a maximum height of 37.5 m and increasing its capacity to some 5.7 million cubic metres.

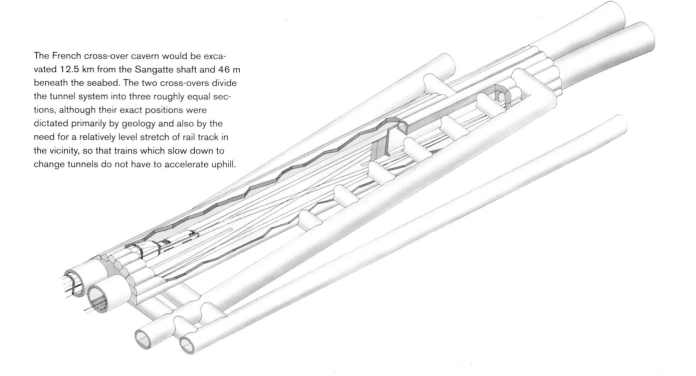

The French cross-over cavern would be excavated 12.5 km from the Sangatte shaft and 46 m beneath the seabed. The two cross-overs divide the tunnel system into three roughly equal sections, although their exact positions were dictated primarily by geology and also by the need for a relatively level stretch of rail track in the vicinity, so that trains which slow down to change tunnels do not have to accelerate uphill.

Work on the French cross-over cavern began in the autumn of 1990.

By November a roadheader was working in the access tunnels. Both of the undersea cross-overs were excavated using conventional mining equipment which could be brought to the site in pieces through the service tunnel.

In October 1990 the task of excavating access tunnels from the service tunnel to the cross-over site began. As on the English side, the service tunnel had been diverted at this point below and to the north of the rail tunnels.

A geologist examining the rock. Investigations by probe drills during August showed that there was water-bearing rock above the site of the cross-over. TML therefore decided to treat this ground with grout, creating an 'umbrella' over the excavations.

Numerous cross-overs and piston relief ducts had to be excavated within the tunnel structure - often by hand.

Although most of the tunnel system was excavated by TBMs and roadheaders, there was still a large amount of hand tunnelling. Every 250 m the two rail tunnels are linked by a piston relief duct designed to prevent pressure building up in front of advancing trains. Every 375 m there is a cross-passage linking all three tunnels, and there are also many technical rooms. These small works offered limited scope for mechanical excavation, and they were dug largely by hand.

On the French side, where there were problems with wet ground, cross-passages were excavated from the rail tunnels towards the service tunnel after all three TBMs had passed. On the English side, cross-passages were excavated from the service tunnel in advance, stopping short before they reached the path of the rail tunnel TBMs.

The beginnings of the entrance to a cross-passage in a French rail tunnel. In the English tunnels, cast-iron segments were inserted where cross-passage openings would be. On the French side, the use of cast iron would have slowed the process of creating a waterproof lining behind the TBM. Instead, after injecting the site of the cross-passage excavations with grout, the concrete segments were stitch-drilled to make an opening.

The cut segments were removed, revealing the grout injected when the segments were placed by the TBM.

Once the opening had been made, miners with pneumatic drills started excavating the cross-passage. A conveyor carried spoil to a waiting construction train.

On the English side, cross-passages were cut within 2 km of the service-tunnel TBM, and the openings were then used for temporary sub-stations and pumping equipment. On the French side, the work was done further back: groups of cross-passages in a tunnel section up to 2 km long were produced by a series of teams, each specialising in one part of the operation.

View through a cross-passage on the English side before fitting out. The figure in the centre is standing in the service tunnel.

Excavating a piston
relief duct. As the
ducts arch over the
service tunnel, the
ends are at an incline.

Piston relief ducts, every 250 m, are needed to prevent pressure building up in front of the trains.

The lined duct is some 23 m long and 2 m in diameter.

A completed duct with its deflector.

The first contact between the English and French undersea service tunnels was a probe drill from the British TBM. The drill, 50 mm in diameter, had been used throughout the drive to find out what kind of ground lay ahead. On 25 October the English TBM stopped its drive and a probe hole 105 m long was drilled.

On 30 October the advancing French TBM met the British probe. The machines had been approaching one another with astonishing accuracy. Later survey calculations showed that the difference in their centrelines was just 358 mm horizontally and 58 mm vertically.

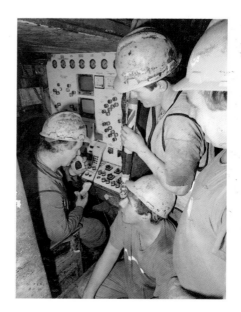

The British and French TBM control cabins on the day of the probe breakthrough.

French and British drives first met underground on 30 October 1990.

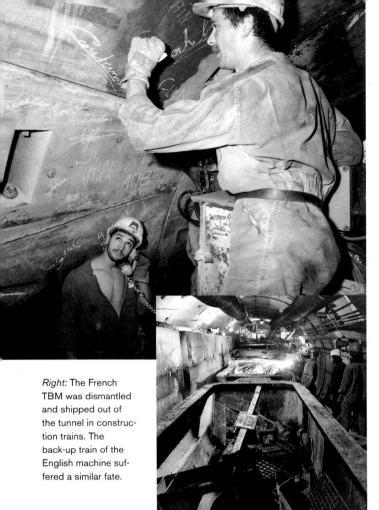

Like other landmark
events in the history of
the Channel Tunnel,
the end of the TBM
drive was marked in
the traditional manner.

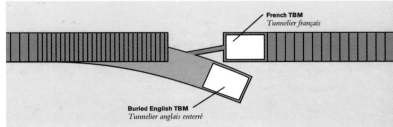

French TBM
Tunnelier français

Buried English TBM
Tunnelier anglais enterré

The service-tunnel TBMs from France and
England were heading straight towards one
another. As the cutterheads were larger than the
lined tunnel, neither could reverse. Instead, the
English machine was steered away to the right
until it was clear of the line of the tunnel. This
short curved section was given a temporary
lining, and miners cut a passage between it and
the French tunnel. Later, the English TBM was
entombed in concrete.

Right: The French
TBM was dismantled
and shipped out of
the tunnel in construc-
tion trains. The
back-up train of the
English machine suf-
fered a similar fate.

By 30 November the
inside of the French
TBM had been cut
away, and workmen
were painting the shell
white for the break-
through ceremonies.
The circular pick-
marks on the working
face are visible
beyond. The break-
through doorway
would be in the centre
of the face.

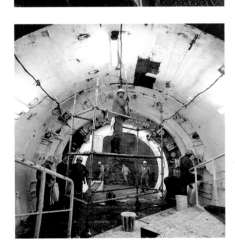

The historic junction
would be watched on
television sets all over
the world.

On 1 December 1990
Philippe Cozette (left)
and Graham Fagg
demolished the last few
centimetres of rock,
creating the first land
route between England
and France for twelve
thousand years.

The ceremony to mark the meeting of the two undersea service-tunnel drives was a historic occasion without precedent.

Above: During the days that followed, TML workmen from France and England met their counterpart for the first time.

Right: On the breakthrough day, personnel and VIPs passed through the breakthrough door to be taken by manriders to the opposite terminal. Waiting frontier officials then added a second historic passport stamp.

Throughout the latter part of 1990,
work on the French terminal forged ahead.

By the end of the summer, a framework 115 m square and 16 m high had risen from the French terminal. This building would be the maintenance centre for Eurotunnel's rolling stock.

Earthworks for road interchanges near Fort Nieulay picked out in the December sunlight.

In early December the cladding was almost complete. The vast hangar had to be equipped in time for the first deliveries of rolling stock.

The French terminal in October 1990, with Calais beyond.

Advances in the terminal installations meant that the drainage system would soon be needed.

Meanwhile, at the English terminal, bridges and trackbeds were under construction.

Opposite: The English terminal in September 1990, with Folkestone and the French coastline beyond.

October: work was in progress on all four overbridges, and trackbeds were beginning to appear between the future platforms.

Before the end of the year the first permanent railway tracks were laid on the Continental Main Line.

Eurotunnel has always made the environment one of its leading concerns.

Eurotunnel acquired much of the escarpment above the English terminal, clearing scrub and dumped rubbish. Grazing was introduced to control coarse grasses. The company joined with other local organisations to carry out similar projects elsewhere in the area.

The Channel Tunnel was built during a period of increasing public concern about the environment. All eyes were focused on this great project, not least in Kent where the works touched on designated areas of great natural beauty or special scientific interest. Eurotunnel and TML were determined from the start to set an example in this field. These pictures represent a tiny fraction of the environmental work which won the respect of many specialist organisations.

A large proportion of the French terminal site consists of landscaped open spaces. In 1993 swans arrived, attracted by the vegetation and fresh water.

In dry weather, roadways on both terminals were sprayed to reduce dust nuisance to surrounding communities.

Summer 1992: mountain bikes on a purpose-built track at Fond de la Forge near Sangatte. When the Sangatte shaft was being excavated, during the first months of the French works, the spoil was brought to an old quarry here. Afterwards, the site was landscaped and planted, and this track was built for a local cycling club.

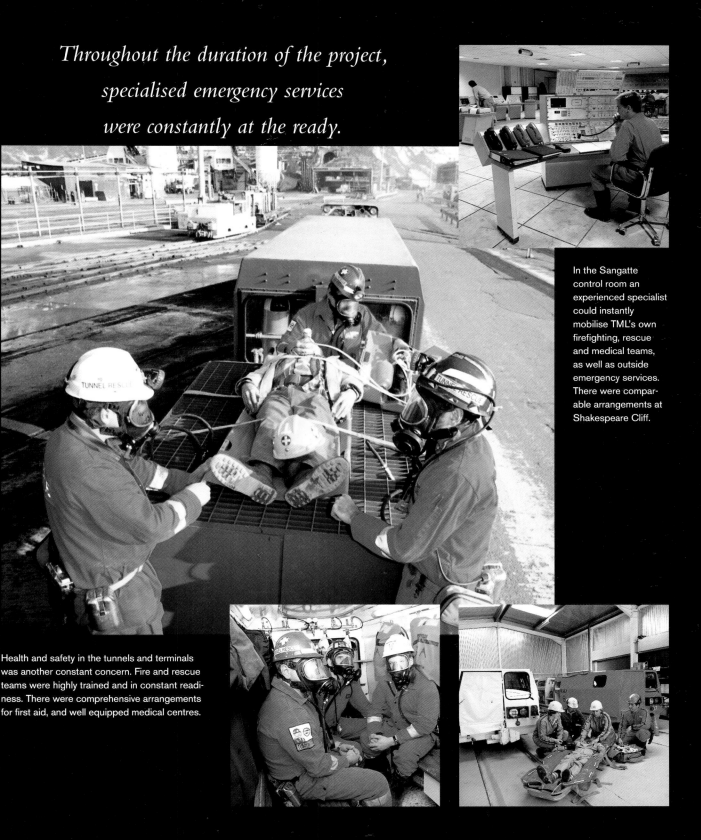

Throughout the duration of the project, specialised emergency services were constantly at the ready.

In the Sangatte control room an experienced specialist could instantly mobilise TML's own firefighting, rescue and medical teams, as well as outside emergency services. There were comparable arrangements at Shakespeare Cliff.

Health and safety in the tunnels and terminals was another constant concern. Fire and rescue teams were highly trained and in constant readiness. There were comprehensive arrangements for first aid, and well equipped medical centres.

CHAPTER 10

January - June 1991

Mid-January:

First tourist-shuttle shells arrive from Canada to be fitted out.

18-24 March:

All-time record week's tunnelling progress: 428 m in the English southern undersea rail tunnel.

23 April:

English northern undersea rail-tunnel drive completed.

9 May:

Isle of Grain segment factory closed.

22 May:

Northern undersea rail tunnel breakthrough linking English and French workings.

28 May:

English southern undersea rail-tunnel drive completed.

24-28 June:

Southern undersea rail tunnel breakthrough linking English and French workings.

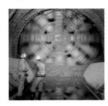

In early March Eurotunnel invited a party of journalists to travel through the service tunnel in construction-railway manriders. The rail journey was not continuous, as the party had to change trains at the junction between British and French works. It was the first time any group representing the French and British public had

were proposed. Without any clear government commitment, the outcome remained uncertain and the earliest possible completion date steadily receded.

Another issue which seized attention in Britain was the risk that rabies might enter the country through the Tunnel. In reality, barriers had been designed into the system

By the end of June all three tunnels had been completed. TML had made history.

been taken through the system, and reports of the journey brought home the scale of the achievement.

By the end of June all three tunnels had been completed. TML had made history. Yet it faced a new challenge: to install the railway track and all the other equipment it needed to operate the transport system.

Elsewhere, attention again focused on the future. There was continuous speculation in the British press about a high-speed link, an issue which had become increasingly complex as different routes and different methods of funding

which make it virtually impossible for an animal to pass through on its own. It would first have to find a way through special fences dug deep into the ground, then it would come to a wide electrified grid. Beyond that, there would be a 50 km walk without food or water, and finally a second set of barriers before it could escape. The risk of smuggling is no different from the risk by other means of cross-Channel transport. Fortunately, the dangers have been greatly reduced by highly successful wildlife vaccination programmes on the European mainland.

Shakespeare Cliff Shaft | TUNNEL PROGRESS CHART | Puits de Sangatte

NORTHERN RAIL TUNNEL — BREAKTHROUGH ◆ JONCTION — TUNNEL FERROVIAIRE NORD
SERVICE TUNNEL — BREAKTHROUGH ◆ JONCTION — GALERIE DE SERVICE
SOUTHERN RAIL TUNNEL — BREAKTHROUGH ◆ JONCTION — TUNNEL FERROVIAIRE SUD

0 km   10   20   30   40   50
50   40   30   20   10   km 0

After the breakthrough celebrations, the English service tunnel was extended along its proper alignment to link up with the French tunnel. These two photographs show the final meeting-point from each side. The shell of the TBM at the end of the French tunnel *(left)* would be lined with segments.

When the junction works were completed, a temporary gate was installed at the frontier between French and English tunnels. Working practices on each side were governed by differing national legislation.

In January 1991 TBM T6 was dismantled at Sangatte, where it had ended its drive, while its back-up train was towed to the Beussingue Trench to be cut into pieces for scrap. Re-usable components were salvaged and offered for sale.

Only one of the seven rail-tunnel TBMs survived the project. This was the record-breaking machine that bored the southern landward tunnel to Holywell. It is seen here on the M20 motorway on its way to Eurotunnel's UK Exhibition Centre, where it was put on display.

During the summer a new shaft 112 m deep and 7.8 m in diameter was excavated between Upper Shakespeare Cliff and the tunnel system. The normal ventilation system would blow air down this shaft into the service tunnel and thence into the rail tunnels through cross-passage vents. A fan duct at Sangatte would perform a similar function at the French end of the tunnel.

Mid-May: the dam at Fond Pignon shortly before the last tunnel spoil arrived.

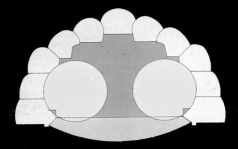

The French cross-over cavern was created by building a huge concrete arch.

Unlike its English counterpart, the French cross-over was excavated after the rail-tunnel TBMs had passed through the site. Moreover, geology made it necessary to use a completely different method of construction. The first step was to build access tunnels around the future cavern. When the rail-tunnel TBMs were clear of the site, an enormous arch 170 m long was created over the tunnels by boring a series of galleries, and filling them with concrete. These formed the 'stones' of the arch. When the arch was complete, the earth beneath it would be removed, exposing the lining segments of the two rail tunnels. Finally, the tunnel linings would be de-molished leaving the enormous cavern empty.

March 1991: dragging cable in the ramp on the south side of the works. The entrance on the right led to one of the galleries, more than 3 m across, which would be excavated then filled with con-crete to form part of the arch. When the service-tunnel drive was completed, 170 people were transferred here to help build the cross-over.

Above: Roadheaders excavated sloping ramps at each side of the site, giving access to the eleven parallel galleries which would form the arch. This photograph taken from behind a road-header shows the four laser beams guiding the machine.

A Lynx roadheader manoeuvring into position at the top of the northern ramp. Note the spoil-conveyor system in the foreground, designed to negotiate not only slopes but corners.

When the lower galleries were excavated, the rail-tunnel linings were exposed. The segment rings were reinforced and closely monitored for movement. Each side gallery was filled with concrete before the next one was bored. Meanwhile, inside the tunnels, the flow of construction trains continued uninterrupted as the TBMs advanced. By the middle of the year nine of the eleven galleries had been excavated and five filled with concrete.

There are pumping stations at each of the three low points in the undersea tunnels. These are 5 km and 15 km from Shakespeare Cliff on the English side, and about 9 km from Sangatte on the French side. The capacity of the pumps was designed for the worst possible case but, in reality, seepage into the tunnels is far lower than was estimated. Separate provision has had to be made to bring water into the pumping stations in order to run the machinery and keep it in good working order!

Three undersea

pumping stations were

built to remove

any seepage.

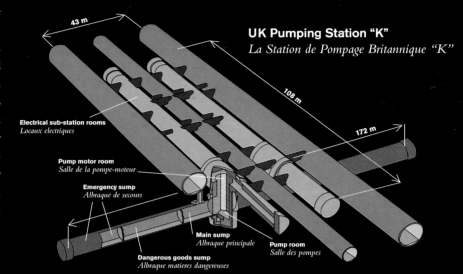

UK Pumping Station "K"
La Station de Pompage Britannique "K"

43 m

108 m

172 m

Electrical sub-station rooms
Locaux electriques

Pump motor room
Salle de la pompe-moteur

Emergency sump
Albraque de secours

Main sump
Albraque principale

Pump room
Salle des pompes

Dangerous goods sump
Albraque matieres dangereuses

Pumping Station K is at the lowest point in the whole of the tunnel system. The layout shown in this TML diagram is similar for all three undersea stations. Long chambers on each side of the service tunnel house electrical and other equipment to drive the pumps, which are in two vertical shafts linked by a sump chamber at right angles to the tunnels. This is 175 m long, 5 m in diameter, and divided into sections for different types of waste.

February 1991: view at the top of the north shaft in Pumping Station K, looking along one of the equipment chambers.

Excavating the sump chamber of Pumping Station K.

February 1992: an engineer inspecting a mass of pipework in Pumping Station K.

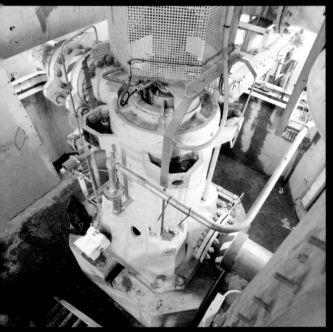

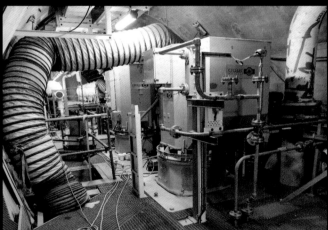

December 1992: electric pump motor and shaft in the pumping station on the French side.

At each of the undersea rail-tunnel junctions, the English TBM dived down below the path of the tunnel and was buried in concrete. Its back-up train was dismantled and taken back to Shakespeare Cliff. The French TBM then advanced to complete the tunnel before being dismantled in its turn.

In May 1991, the northern rail tunnel was complete - a historic moment.

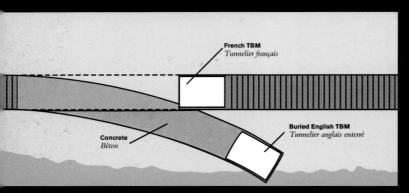

French TBM
Tunnelier français

Concrete
Béton

Buried English TBM
Tunnelier anglais enterré

10 May: a chaotic scene as the TBM back-up train was dismantled.

The northern rail-tunnel TBM on the English side built its last ring of lining segments on 23 April, eight weeks ahead of schedule. It was then driven in a steep dive for 66 m, stopping finally on 4 May. Two days later, as this photograph shows, all but the top of the gripper section had disappeared under a sea of concrete.

21 May: the French TBM began to drive into the sloping tunnel left by the English machine, now buried directly underneath it. The sloping tunnel had been lined with a weak concrete mix.

22 May: the first railway tunnel between Britain and France was completed in front of a large crowd of spectators.

The English southern rail-tunnel TBM built its last lining ring on 28 May and completed its dive on 8 June. In its last hours, the build area was spattered with the shotcrete used to create a temporary tunnel lining.

Under the back-up train.

17 June: concrete nearing the top of the gripper section.

25 June: two spectators in the English tunnel shake hands as the French TBM grinds forward to complete 150 km of tunnel system.

The last breakthrough of all:
southern undersea rail tunnel
24-28 June 1991

28 June: the last break-through ceremony, almost exactly half way between Shakespeare Cliff and the Sangatte shaft, was the climax of a magnificent tunnelling achievement. All the delays suffered during the early months had been recovered, and this final junction took place two days ahead of the schedule announced in 1985.

Concrete trackbed castings mark out the line of the future platforms.

Sand fill was placed between the trackbed castings to build up the level of the platforms.

March: laying asphalt on the deck of an over-bridge. These bridges now saw a considerable volume of traffic because they offered the only convenient route from one side of the terminal to the other.

With the overbridges already in action, the French terminal was beginning to take shape.

The Fort Nieulay interchange would be graced by an elegant viaduct in the form of a 'Y'.

Late April: staircases are delivered to the growing control tower. This building on the hillside west of the platform area would house the road-traffic control centre for the terminal and the reserve control centre for the railway system.

The delivery of the first shuttle wagon components
marked the start of a new phase
in the Channel Tunnel's construction.

On 11 February the English terminal was transformed by snow: the first heavy fall since work began.

During the spring the main substation on the English terminal began to take shape. This would draw power at 123,000 volts from the national grid and convert it to the voltages needed in the tunnels and terminal.

In early January 1991 the first stainless-steel shells for Eurotunnel's shuttle wagons arrived in Zeebrugge on board the 'Federal Ottawa'. They were built by Bombardier in Canada.

The next stage of their journey was by canal barge to Bruges, where they would be fitted-out by BN, another company in the Bombardier group.

CHAPTER 11

15 July:

Start of standard-gauge tracklaying in English rail tunnels.

15 August:

English main sub-station connected to the national grid.

23 October:

The UK cross-over receives the British Construction Industry Award for the year's finest achievement in civil engineering.

6 November:

Eurotunnel signs a long-term loan facility for £200 million with the European Coal and Steel Community.

25 November:

Franco-British protocol on tunnel frontier controls.

4 December:

First shuttle-locomotive shell leaves Qualter Hall to be fitted out at Loughborough.

July – December 1991

Following completion of the three tunnels as well as most of the civil engineering work on the terminals, the entire nature of the project changed. The segment and spoil trains were replaced by trains fitted with special rigs such as those gressed steadily shift by shift. Each fit-out task had to be repeated along the full 50 km length of the system. Above ground, there was no further segment manufacture, and spoil disposal at Shakespeare Cliff and Fond Pignon had

> *Each fit-out task had to be repeated along the full 50 km length of the system.*

used to put pipes or cable in position. While the tunnelling work had been carried out by TML's own labour force, most of the mechanical and electrical fixed equipment was installed by specialist subcontractors. The total number of people working on the project remained the same: around 8,000 on the UK side and 5,700 on the French side, but the proportion of labour employed directly by TML was falling.

Below ground, the tunnels became a series of isolated worksites which pro-

ceased. The equipment used for these purposes was being dismantled.

When the first rolling stock arrived, the public's perception of the tunnel as a construction project began to fade, to be replaced gradually by the perception of a cross-Channel transport system. Comment focused more sharply on potential competition with the ferries, on the future of the Channel ports, and on the opportunities that the Tunnel would create, particularly in the depressed regions of northern France.

By July, grass was beginning to grow above the cut-and-cover tunnels at Holywell. In the foreground, the TBM reception chambers had been roofed over. They too would shortly disappear.

Checking the integrity of welds in the cross-over steelwork.

August: the permanent concrete lining of the UK cross-over had been cast. It is about 90 cm thick at the crown and up to 120 cm thick at the sides. The steel plates high up on the walls in the foreground form part of the mounting for the girder structure which supports giant sliding doors.

In early October work began dismantling the rail-tunnel linings in the French cross-over and clearing away the central bench of rock between them.

The crown of the French cross-over cavern was excavated at one end before the last gallery had been filled at the other. The roadheader seen here in late August was manoeuvring high up under the roof of the arch.

Right: Mechanical diggers removing rock from the crown of the cavern. The two rail tunnels lie beneath.

Left: By early September all eleven galleries making up the roof of the cross-over had been excavated and filled. This view shows a wall of shuttering closing off a section of one of the last galleries. Concrete was pumped through pipes into the space behind.

Saint Barbara, the patron saint of miners, was not forgotten. Her niche beneath the cross-over was regularly decorated with flowers.

During December the structure of the cavern was completed by excavating the floor and laying a thick concrete invert.

All three tunnels were roofed over where they crossed the Sangatte shaft. Likewise, the sides and roofs of the huge TBM chambers at Shakespeare Cliff were walled and back-filled to match the size of the tunnels.

The base of the Sangatte shaft had to be weighted down with concrete. When the TBM drives were over, the spoil-treatment machinery was dismantled and a thousand tonnes of equipment was put on sale. The next task was to 'ballast' the shaft. This would prevent it floating like a giant oil drum when the ground water eventually returns to its natural level. Calculations showed that it was necessary to weigh down the base of the shaft with 130,000 tonnes of concrete.

Doors at the outer ends of each cross-passage isolate the service tunnel from the rail tunnels. If a shuttle train stops, there will be at least two of these safety exits along its length. The ventilation system pumps huge amounts of fresh air into the service tunnel. The air passes at intervals through the cross-passages into the rail tunnels. The direction and strength of this airflow would prevent smoke from a tunnel fire entering the cross-passage, which is therefore a safe haven.

One of the doors in position. They have been designed to withstand the air pressure created by passing trains and to provide an effective fire barrier. Yet they open easily in either powered or manual modes.

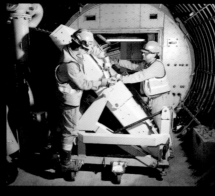

Special machines installed a valve in every piston-relief duct. In an emergency, the valves could be closed in 30 seconds, preventing air or smoke passing from one rail tunnel to the other.

The fixed equipment incorporated
many new design and safety features.

Tracklaying on the English terminal began in November 1990 and on the French side in December. The railway track gauge, 1.435 m, is the same in both countries, although the loading gauge (the maximum height and width of wagons) is different. However, steel rails used in the Eurotunnel system are of the heavy-duty European type (60 kg/m) never previously employed in Britain. This is because the tunnel tracks will ultimately carry a greater load than any other railway in the world. The 95 km of track laid in the two terminals includes mill-hardened rails to reduce wear on the loops, and some extremely long points which allow trains to change tracks at speed. At each terminal there is a complex network of sidings and maintenance areas in addition to the shuttle loop, platforms and Continental Main Line.

Installing firemain in the service tunnel. There is far more safety equipment available than in most stretches of railway track above ground. The high-pressure firemain in the service tunnel is supplied from reservoirs at Sangatte, Shakespeare Cliff and both portals. The cross-passages contain, on each side, distribution pipework and foam-making equipment to supply hydrants in the rail tunnels.

The fire hydrants have two valves, one to fit hoses used by the French fire service and the other to fit hoses used by the British.

Laying track for the shuttle loop at the French terminal, March 1991.

Everywhere, the track geometry was rigorously checked.

A ballast train and ballast adjuster on the shuttle loop at the French terminal, April 1991.

Trackwork in the shuttle loop, at the English terminal, August 1991.

By July 1991 the bridges, ramps and trackbeds in the French terminal platform area were all in place. In this aerial view the 300 m long over-bridges seem to be longer than required. The extra space on each side will allow the number of platforms to be doubled as traffic levels increase.

The English terminal: shuttles will enter the platforms at the end farthest from the camera. The two bridges at the rear are for vehicles boarding the shuttles, while the exit bridges are in the foreground. As in France, there is provision to add extra platforms without extending the bridges. Note also the control building, which houses both the main railway control centre and the control centre for road vehicles on the terminal.

October: the first rail track in the platform area. The French terminal, hitherto an isolated building site, would soon be a vital part of an international railway system.

During the summer the main electrical substations close to the French and English portals were completed.

The 240 MVA British substation was energised on August 1. It provides power for the UK installations and half the tunnel system.

The French main substation beside the Beussingue Trench was energised on 21 November. It provides power to the French half of the tunnels and the terminal installations. In the event of a power failure on one side of the Channel, the tunnels can be supplied entirely by the other substation.

After the tracklaying, teams began erecting the masts and overhead catenary wires from which trains would draw electrical power throughout the Eurotunnel system. In the platform area of the French terminal, the catenary wires were suspended from a series of elegant structures bridging the platforms.

Building the Trans-Manche Super Trains. In 1988 the British, French and Belgian railways formed a consortium to order special high-speed passenger trains for services through the Channel Tunnel. The tender was won by an international consortium which included GEC, Alsthom, and other leading specialists in all three countries. The mechanical design of the new trains was based on the successful French TGV, adapted to the smaller British loading gauge. The electrical equipment, however, needed to be much more complex. As the trains would run on three national railway systems the locomotives had to cope with three different voltages supplied either by overhead catenary or third rail.

Components for the shuttle trains came from many countries. Here, an engineer at the ABB factory in Tramont-Oerlikon in Switzerland studies the control box circuit for a shuttle locomotive.

CHAPTER 12

January – June 1992

Work to strip out pipework and cabling used during the construction phase went hand in hand with the installation of permanent fixed equipment. This created a heavy demand for transport at a time when movements were handicapped by trackwork in the rail tunnels. The logistics of the project had never been more complicated.

By the end of June most of the pipework in the tunnels for the cooling and firemain systems had been installed, as well as a large proportion of electric cable and catenary. Trackwork, an enormous undertaking, progressed steadily.

Despite the scale and importance of these tasks, their nature attracted little public interest. The tunnels seemed to have lost much of their glamour at a moment when they were, in reality, becoming much more interesting. The terminals, too, were coming to life as TML and Eurotunnel staff refined the future operating procedures. When the system opened, the public would see far

In May, the two construction railways were briefly linked so that a manrider could take HRH The Duke of Edinburgh through the system from England to France.

more of the terminals than the tunnels.

In May, the two construction railways were briefly linked so that a manrider could take HRH The Duke of Edinburgh through the system from England to France. This was the first and only occasion that a through train travelled the full length of the construction railways. The Duke's visit, which included several stops to see work in progress, left a lasting impression on his hosts, not least in the second part of the journey where he switched to speaking fluent French.

Like the tunnel-lining segments, sleeper blocks contain steel reinforcement.

340,000 sleeper blocks were made at the Sangatte precast factory.

A technician checking the geometry of a sleeper block. Variations as small as 1 or 2 mm in the 100 kg casting could lead to rejection.

Before standard-gauge tracklaying could begin, the narrow gauge construction-railway tracks had to be removed. In the English rail tunnels, this was done by a moving crane which ran along the ledge moulded into each side of the tunnel lining.

The shingle ballast on which rail tracks are normally laid is not quite rigid. This elasticity greatly reduces the mechanical stress caused when a heavy train passes at speed. Although the trackbed in the tunnels is made of concrete, the Sonneville track design achieves a similar effect by placing impact-absorbing pads under the concrete sleeper-blocks. The pads and sleeper-blocks are enclosed in rubber 'boots' and attached to the rail before it is laid.

Some 340,000 sleeper-blocks were produced to exacting standards in the Sangatte precast factory. Since tracklaying took place simultaneously on the English and French sides, 180,000 blocks were loaded on lorries and taken to the UK by ferry.

Rails 180 m long were mounted on sleeper-blocks then stockpiled under gantries, which would load them onto special tracklaying trains.

the French side a machine nicknamed the
Diplodocus' was armed with a grab of 5 cubic
metres' capacity which removed debris from the
tunnel floor.

The 60 m long Diplodocus also lifted the
construction rails and their supporting girders.

The rail tunnels had to be completely clean
before the first stage of the concrete trackbed
could be laid. This machine followed the
Diplodocus, scouring the surface of the linings
with high-pressure water jets.

*One hundred kilometers
of tunnel had to be
prepared for the
tracklaying teams.*

In the English rail tunnels, the shingle ballast
under the construction tracks had to be
removed.

When the tunnel was clean, concrete was poured to form a floor. This incorporated a central drainpipe, seen *(above)* held in position on transverse supports.

Thousands of tonnes of concrete had to be poured to make a floor in the rail tunnels.

A tracklaying train a the head of the Beussingue Trench its way to the tunne Despite their streng the four 180 m trac strings can be seer bending on the cur The train also carrie the gantries used to lay the track.

...eyond the track
...ready laid is a
...emporary section
...ounted on wheels
...hich run along the
...oncrete floor. At the
...eginning of each
...ycle this is joined to
...e last rails laid,
...xtending the track
...ong the tunnel. The
...acklaying train then
...oves forward onto it.

The feet of the gantries on the track-laying train extend, lifting the gantries with two rail strings off the train. The train itself then moves back off the temporary section, which will be disconnected and towed forwards to leave the trackbed clear.

When the gantry arms are raised the track-laying train will move forward, collect the gantries, and begin the whole process again.

The track strings are lowered. Before they are finally positioned, spacers will be fitted to ensure the correct gauge. The temporary track section (bottom right) will then be attached.

Before the sleeper-blocks were concreted into position, they were positioned with great accuracy in relation both to the tunnel and to the preceding string of track. Precise work at this stage would reduce track noise, greatly enhance ride quality, and prolong the life of the rails. Subsequent checks showed that the track geometry achieved in the Channel Tunnel is better even than on the French TGV lines.

Concrete was poured under and around the sleeper blocks, locking them in position. The rubber boots make it possible to replace any block that becomes damaged.

The Channel Tunnel Trackwork Group, an Anglo-French consortium, used highly sophisticated 2,000 tonne trains to make concrete in the tunnels. These were, in effect, mobile batching plants delivering up to 80 cubic metres of concrete an hour.

The last stage was to build walkways along each side of the rail tunnels. In the English tunnels these incorporated the ledges cast in the tunnel linings. Similar ledges were added on the French side. The walkways were made up of precast sections which were lowered into position from works trains.

Below: At Shakespeare Cliff a complication arose that had no equivalent in France. Construction trains from the pithead had to cross the southern rail tunnel on their way to the service tunnel. To make this possible, an unusual swing bridge was built at the bottom of Adit A2.

For a while, standard-gauge track in the rail tunnels coexisted with the 90 cm gauge construction railway.

Works trains on the English terminal. Once the standard-gauge tracks were laid, the flexibility of the double-track construction railway was lost. Different fixed-equipment teams needed access to the tunnels, but the work sites nearest the portals blocked everything beyond them inside the tunnel for the duration of the shift. The movements of different work-trains required very careful planning, as the only two-way traffic was in the service tunnel, where the construction railway was still in place.

A standard-gauge diesel locomotive fitted with exhaust scrubbers for work in the tunnels. The part-finished structure in the background is the English maintenance building, much smaller than the main facility in France.

In May the trackwork of the diamond crossing in the UK undersea cross-over was being prepared. Note the wooden sleepers under the points, and the overhead structure which would support the sliding doors separating the tunnels.

Above: There is a cross-over at each end of the Tunnel. In France it is in the Beussingue Trench just outside the portal. At the English terminal there was much less space so the two-part cross-over is in the Tunnel. One part is close to the portal and the other under Holywell. In this view of the Holywell cross-over, the yellow doors of the cross-tunnel are standing open. In normal operation, when the cross-over is not in use, they are closed.

By April 1992 the three tunnels across the base of the Sangatte shaft were entirely covered. A personnel lift *(left)* was the only faint reminder of the past. Steel reinforcement marked the beginning of massive ducts being built for the permanent ventilation systems, one of the key installations at Sangatte.

The central section of the French cross-over floor was laid at the beginning of 1992. Like its English equivalent it would carry a diamond crossing and sliding doors.

Technical rooms and a central corridor were being built high up under the cross-over roof. They would form part of the unseen workings of the Channel Tunnel transport system.

By late April the French cross-over had changed beyond recognition. Dividing walls had been built at each end of the cavern and the overhead steelwork was in place.

As the number of trains increases, the temperature will rise, so a cooling system has been installed.

The four chillers at Lower Shakespeare Cliff were delivered at the end of April 1992. They are seen here soon afterwards. Their combined capacity is 7.65 megawatts, slightly higher than the four chillers at Sangatte.

Trains and equipment in the tunnels all use energy. This presents a problem because most of it is eventually transformed, in one way or another, into heat. As the number of trains increases, the temperature in the rail tunnels could rise beyond an acceptable level. An immense cooling system has therefore been installed. When the temperature reaches a certain point, chilled water will be pumped through pipes in the rail tunnels. A plant at Lower Shakespeare Cliff will supply four loops, one in the landward and one in the undersea section of each rail tunnel. A second plant at Sangatte will supply loops in the two undersea tunnels, and a single loop for the short landward tunnels

Beside the building housing the chillers are dry-air coolers, so called because the water being cooled circulates in pipes rather than in the open. The cheerful paintwork of this cooler at Sangatte gives it a decidedly French air, compared to its subdued English counterpart at Lower Shakespeare Cliff.

At the French and English tunnel portals, lengths of cooling pipe were welded together before being taken into the tunnels.

Special trains with robotic arms transported the long sections of pipe into the tunnels and placed them in their brackets on the walls. Welding the sections together in the confined space available called for the skills of a contortionist. Afterwards the welds were sandblasted and checked with X-ray equipment.

The end of the cooling loop in the northern landward rail tunnel on the English side. This photograph had the longest time-exposure used in the tunnel: 40 minutes at F45 using a 500 mm lens.

Left: In the spring of 1992 a new building was rapidly taking shape on the slope above the platform area of the French terminal. This was the future operating headquarters of the Eurotunnel transport system. Staff would begin to move in later that year.

Eurotunnel's shuttle wagons are the world's largest rolling stock. This is reflected in the proportions of the maintenance building on the French terminal. When fitted out, its huge entrance doors would conceal a mass of equipment, including a 25-tonne overhead crane lifting to a height of 12 m.

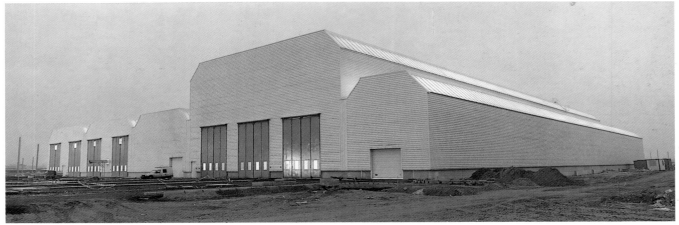

In January 1992 much of the interior was still empty except for a line of jacks capable of lifting up to three shuttle wagons at a time.

During the spring of 1992 the Fort Nieulay interchange began to take its final form. While the carriageways were prepared for surfacing, excavators began to turn the centre of the interchange into an artificial lake 400 m in diameter.

The spirit of the catenary masts in the platform area is reflected in the spreading canopies of the toll plaza. The structures are more solid than they look: each section, 18 m across, weighs 40 tonnes.

Left: Erecting toll canopies at the entrance to the English terminal. While the terminals are the two ends of a single system, they are in different countries. Rather than attempting a uniform architectural approach on both sides of the Channel, the structures and buildings were designed to complement their very different settings.

Right: The striking fabric roof over the atrium of the passenger terminal building had been raised into position the previous November. Manufactured in America, such roofs are more often found in the Middle East than in England.

Some travellers will hurry through, others will find the services they need.

In March the structure of the passenger terminal building was nearing completion. Travellers with a few minutes to spare will find a wide range of facilities there, including restaurants, shops, information, and duty-free stores.

Half of the 216 shuttle-wagon shells were delivered to ANF at Crespin in France, where they were fitted with upper decks. This enables the wagons to carry ten cars rather than five. Vehicles higher than 1.85 m travel in the single-deck shuttles, which are able to carry large coaches.

Insulating the upper deck of a shuttle wagon. The air-conditioned interior is protected against noise, heat and fire.

Installing the interior lining of a single-deck shuttle wagon at BN's factory in Bruges.

The nine club cars to be used by freight drivers were built in Italy by the Breda-Fiat consortium. They are based on rolling stock in service between Rome and Florence, with specially adapted interiors finished to first-class passenger standards.

Electricians working on cable looms under a shuttle wagon, each of which has some 50 km of wiring.

The railway system through the tunnel is modern, fast, and exceptionally safe.

On 29 April the first rolling stock was delivered: one of 33 loading wagons for the HGV (heavy goods vehicle) shuttles. It had been transported to the English terminal by road from the Fiat works at Savigliano in Italy. The two sides fold down onto the platform to provide a roadway for lorries boarding or driving off the shuttle.

At the Krupp Mak works in Germany one of Eurotunnel's five diesel locomotives begins to take shape. These will be used for shunting at the terminals but, in an emergency, they could be sent to pull a disabled train out of the tunnel.

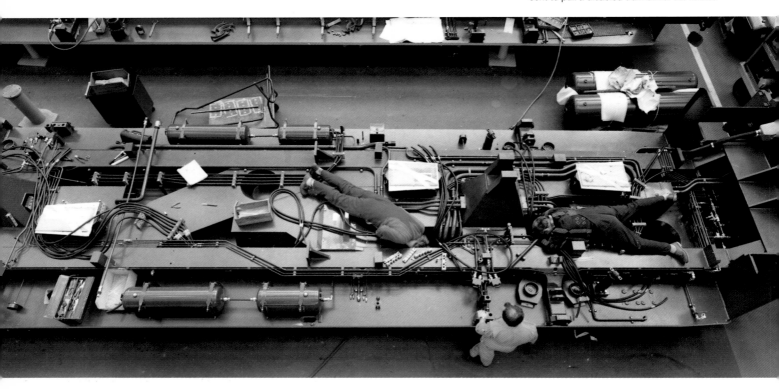

In England, the steel shells of the 76 shuttle loco-motives were built by Qualter Hall at Barnsley before transfer to the Brush Traction works at Loughborough for fitting out with propulsion equipment made by ABB in Switzerland.

There was rigorous and exhaustive testing at every stage in the development of the Channel Tunnel and its equipment. Here, a locomotive shell is subjected to stress at the British Rail Research facility in Derby.

CHAPTER 13

8 July:

Announcement that Eurotunnel's cross-Channel service for road vehicles would be called 'Le Shuttle'.

28 July:

The first two HGV carriers arrive at the English terminal.

31 July:

Tracklaying completed in the southern English rail tunnels.

11 August:

New Eurotunnel Exhibition Centre opened, overlooking the French terminal.

26 November:

TGV Nord track linked to the trackwork of the French terminal.

30 November:

Demarcation of the Anglo-French frontier under the Channel.

14 December:

First electric shuttle locomotive delivered to the French terminal.

15 December:

First diesel locomotive delivered to the French terminal.

July – December 1992

By the end of the year, the tunnels and terminals were visibly nearing completion. Much of the work that remained was highly technical, such as the installation and commissioning of complex signalling, control and communication systems.

As the start of operations approached, Eurotunnel was transforming itself into an operating company. The expanding commercial department would be responsible for promoting and selling tickets for the shuttle service, as well as the management of the passenger-service buildings and other activities producing revenue. The operations department had to recruit and train all the personnel needed to run the terminals, tunnels, and railway system. Senior managers already in place were trained by TML or the equipment suppliers. They then designed the procedures and training courses for the staff who would be recruited closer to opening. Every department faced unique challenges in this start-up process. In addition to the terminal staff and train crew who would deal directly with the public, a host of technical posts were filled. The tunnel systems would need to be operated and maintained. There was recruitment from transport operations elsewhere, and many technical staff joined Eurotunnel from TML. They would help to run the system they had built. TML personnel also joined Eurotunnel to be retrained. Thus Philippe Cozette, the French tunnel worker chosen by ballot to make the first breakthrough in December 1990, moved across to Eurotunnel to become a shuttle-train driver.

Eurotunnel was transforming itself into an operating company.

On 30 November the Anglo-French land frontier was officially marked in a ceremony beneath the Channel.

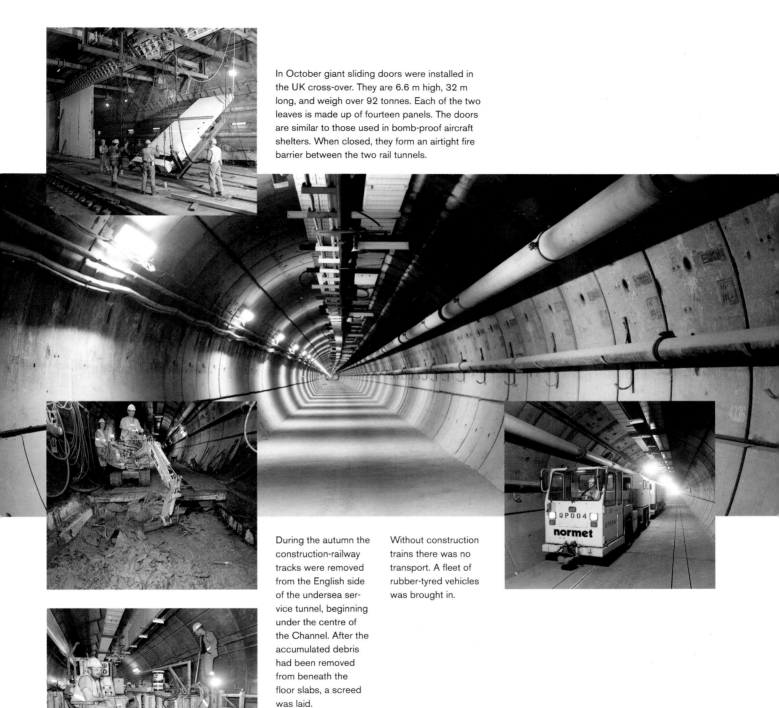

In October giant sliding doors were installed in the UK cross-over. They are 6.6 m high, 32 m long, and weigh over 92 tonnes. Each of the two leaves is made up of fourteen panels. The doors are similar to those used in bomb-proof aircraft shelters. When closed, they form an airtight fire barrier between the two rail tunnels.

During the autumn the construction-railway tracks were removed from the English side of the undersea service tunnel, beginning under the centre of the Channel. After the accumulated debris had been removed from beneath the floor slabs, a screed was laid.

Without construction trains there was no transport. A fleet of rubber-tyred vehicles was brought in.

In November work began laying the permanent service-tunnel floor on the French side.

Near the cross-overs, flights of stairs link the rail-tunnel cross-passages to the service tunnel, diverted downwards and to the north of the rail tunnels in the vicinity of the cross-over.

By the end of August the tracks in the northern French rail tunnel had reached the cross-over. In October, when the line was completed to the junction with the British works, the tracklaying equipment was transferred to the southern tunnel.

The power of the ventilation systems far exceeds the requirement. They will never be turned off.

January 1992: SVS fans negotiating the narrow road tunnel down to Lower Shakespeare Cliff.

The normal ventilation system blows 161 cubic metres of fresh air a second into the full length of the rail tunnels via the service tunnel and cross-passages. There is also an extremely powerful supplementary ventilation system (SVS) for use in an emergency. Fans at each end of the under-sea section can blow air into the rail tunnels or suck it out. The flow rates are 300 cubic metres a second at Lower Shakespeare Cliff and 260 cubic metres a second at Sangatte. This system would make it possible to clear the tunnels of smoke or noxious fumes very rapidly.

April 1992: assembling the fans.

Air from the SVS fans, cooling loops, firemain and other services all go from Lower Shakespeare Cliff to the tunnel system through Adit A2. The five sets of construction-railway tracks have gone, and the adit is now clean and relatively quiet.

Viewed from outside or inside the housing, the SVS fans are very large indeed.

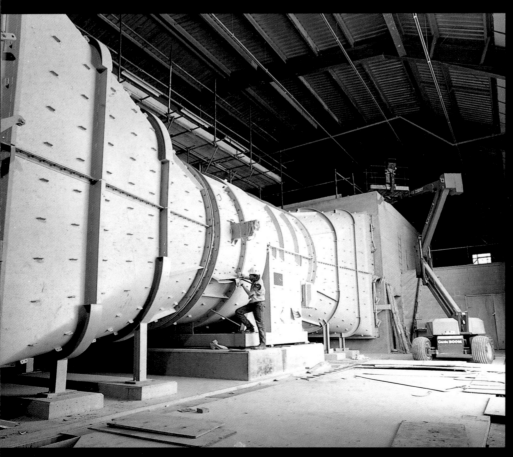

A view down into the Sangatte shaft in late October. The ducting for the normal ventilation system can be seen top left, while the larger SVS ducting, lower left, is still incomplete. Pipework for the cooling loops and other services is visible on the right.

By April 1993 the permanent installations at Sangatte would be complete. In the centre is the chiller building, with air coolers in the foreground. The normal ventilation building and ducting is on the left, and the SVS on the right. The cylindrical tank is a firemain reservoir. The remainder of the shafthead buildings would be demolished.

Insulation work on the fan housings at Sangatte.

Everything in the tunnel, from trains to light fittings, is powered by electricity.

Special works trains laid cable into the trays high up on the side of the tunnels.

Electricity supplies everything in the Channel tunnel from trains to some 20,000 light fittings. In addition to the main sub-stations near each portal (and 23 further substations on the terminals) there are fourteen pairs of substations in the tunnels, which contain a total of 148 electrical rooms. Everywhere, systems are backed up so that if one fails another takes over. If the English supply fails, the tunnels can be powered from France, and vice-versa.

If both national supplies fail, essential equipment underground will be supplied from emergency generators on constant standby at Sangatte and Shakespeare Cliff.

In addition to electricity supply there are communications systems, signalling systems, and a host of monitoring and safety systems such as smoke detectors. Installing electrical equipment on this scale was an enormous task.

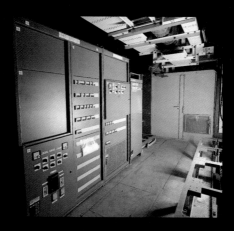

Tunnels similar to
cross-passages
contain technical
rooms for the major
electrical systems.

Electrical teams
worked countless
shifts installing equip-
ment such as perma-
nent lighting along
150 km of tunnel.

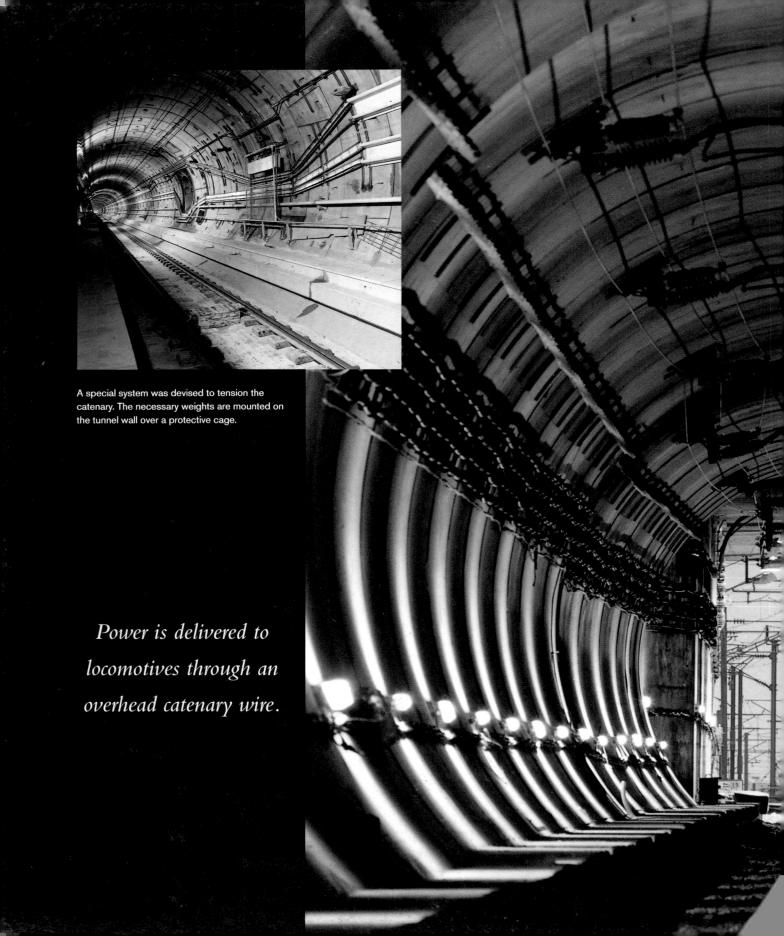

A special system was devised to tension the catenary. The necessary weights are mounted on the tunnel wall over a protective cage.

Power is delivered to locomotives through an overhead catenary wire.

The catenary, which runs the length of the two 50 km rail tunnels, involved fixing six wires on special supports high up in the roof. The contact wire zig-zags so as to wear the pantograph on the locomotives evenly.

By the end of 1992,
the structures on the terminals
were almost all complete.

During the autumn the canopies on the French toll plaza were completed. Work began on the toll-booths and frontier-control posts.

The English Terminal on a November evening.

In September 1992 the interchange at Fort Nieulay was ready for use. It provides a fitting entrance to the terminal, which is not only the 'gateway' to Britain but also a popular tourist attraction.

Wind fences have been erected in exposed places on both terminals so that the shuttle service can operate in stormy weather.

On 28 July the first two HGV shuttle wagons arrived at the Folkestone terminal, having travelled by road from Italy. The semi-open design makes it possible for the wagon to carry a 44 tonne lorry without exceeding the permissable axle loading.

A month after the first two HGV wagons reached England, 24 further wagons were unloaded at the Port of Calais and taken by road to the French terminal. This was almost enough to make up a freight shuttle, which would have 28 HGV carriers.

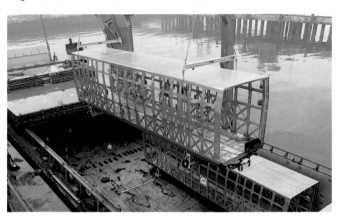

The future would belong to the giant shuttle wagons, centre. In October, however, the English Terminal sidings were still packed with tunnel works trains.

On arrival in the maintenance building, the wagons were lifted off the road transporters by giant jacks, then lowered onto railway bogies.

Pits beneath railway tracks in the maintenance building make it easy to work underneath rolling stock. More than 500 units in the shuttle fleet had to be checked and commissioned before they could enter service.

In October the first amenity coach for HGV drivers arrived from Italy. Meals are provided during the cross-Channel journey, which qualifies as a driver's statutory break.

At the Brush works in Loughborough on 12 December the first shuttle locomotive to be delivered was covered with protective sheeting before setting off to Dover by road.

Even without their bogies, the locomotives are too big to travel on the British Rail network, or, indeed, on a minor road.

The locomotives suffered the indignity of having to make their first Channel crossing by ferry!

The end of one journey and the beginning of another: inside the maintenance building the locomotive bodies were transferred onto their bogies.

In the future, these orange Transmanche Super Trains would run to Paris on the same track as the grey-liveried TGV Nord. An entirely new high-speed line has been built between Paris and the Tunnel, connecting with other major routes at Lille.

At the beginning of December the first two diesel loco-motives arrived at the French terminal. They are the most powerful of their type in the world, and quickly proved their worth.

CHAPTER 14

January – June 1993

11 January:

Eurotunnel's Operating Headquarters at the French terminal is officially opened.

29 January:

Sir Christopher Mallaby travels through the tunnel to take up his appointment as British Ambassador in Paris.

3 February:

Eurotunnel's command and procedure exercises, used to train railway and terminal controllers, win a National Training Award.

12 March:

The first passenger train passes through the tunnel, with a party of guests from the European Investment Bank.

April:

Tunnel tracklaying completed.

18 May:

The first section of the TGV Nord is inaugurated, between Paris and Arras.

June:

The first tourist shuttle wagons are delivered to the French terminal.

20 June:

The first Eurostar passenger train passes through the tunnel.

In the eyes of the press, the first half of 1993 was clouded by negotiations between Eurotunnel and TML about rising project costs. On the sites, however, there was relentless progress as teams from the two companies worked to bring the giant project to completion. The tasks were extremely complex, and there was increasing uncertainty about the date on which services could begin.

One by one the remaining technical questions were resolved. Meanwhile, the commissioning process moved forward. First, every individual item of equipment had to be tested in isolation. Then complete subsystems would be tested, and so on, until it was certain that the entire system was working properly.

During the spring, landscaping work and tree planting on the construction sites wrought a dramatic change in their

> *During the spring, landscaping work and tree planting on the construction sites wrought a dramatic change in their appearance.*

appearance. Mud gave way to grass and, as the temporary construction offices and workshops were dismantled, there was a tangible feeling of nostalgia. Most of TML's construction workers and a large proportion of the engineers had already left. A great project was coming to an end.

Looking over the Fort Nieulay interchange
towards the French terminal.

17 April: the last miners to work in the English tunnels pose for a group photograph. Many were skilled specialists in tunnelling work who move all over the world from one project to another. On the French side, by contrast, the project recruited largely from the local labour market. TML invested heavily in training, leaving much of its workforce better qualified for the future.

During the later stages of the work, old British Rail passenger coaches were used to transport people into the tunnels.

In April the last Alimak personnel hoist was removed.

As at Sangatte, the Lower Shakespeare Cliff pithead installations had to be dismantled so that the site could be remodelled. The Demag cranes, which had handled so many thousands of tonnes of segments and materials, disappeared one by one.

The construction railway shrunk steadily until finally, at the beginning of May, the last tracks were removed from Adit A1.

The whole of the land platform at Lower Shakespeare Cliff was to be landscaped. The only permanent structures would be the cooling, firemain and supplementary ventilation installations at the eastern end.

The fans for the Normal Ventilation System had been lowered into their shaft at Upper Shakespeare Cliff in October. By January 1993 the scale of the installation was apparent. Similar fans had been installed at Sangatte.

Pipes from the cooling plant at Sangatte entering the tunnels at the base of the shaft.

9 January 1993: French tracklaying reaches the end of the English track in the southern rail tunnel.

A works train at the French portal.

In the French tunnels, the narrow-gauge manriders were replaced with rolling stock dating from the 1950s. The unusual position of the driver's cabin earned these trains the nickname 'Picassos'.

Eurotunnel's commercial staff had now moved from London to the Operating Headquarters over-looking the platform area on the French terminal.

Thousands of trees and shrubs have been planted on the terminals.

The entrance to the English terminal is a slip road from the M20 motorway, which leads to a row of tollbooths. The second group of canopies covers the customs and frontier-control area. Aerial views show clearly how limited was the space available compared to the terminal in France.

The control building on the English terminal dominates the site. The controllers responsible for road-traffic movements therefore have an excellent view. In practice this is not essential for their work, which is highly automated. They must keep traffic moving day and night in all weathers, even in the notorious Channel fogs!

The 'view' in the Railway Control Centre was to be no less impressive: a panoramic mimic panel representing the entire track system. Work on the panel supports had begun in January 1993.

Before starting to operate the system, Eurotunnel had to recruit and train a large staff in a wide variety of functions. For example, simulators such as this were installed on both terminals for shuttle-locomotive drivers.

Language training has been a notable element in the programme from a very early stage. Although the transport system links two countries, it has to be run as a single entity. Therefore Eurotunnel staff are not segregated into French and British sections: even in areas which may appear distinct, such as the operation of the two terminals, there is very close collaboration between staff on each side.

Special vehicles, long but narrow, were developed for use in the service tunnel. As they cannot turn round there is a cab at each end. The central section is an interchangeable container, with versions available for maintenance, firefighting, and ambulance duties. The service tunnel is patrolled constantly, and first-response emergency services are never more than 15 minutes from any point. At speeds up to 50 km/hour the risk of a head-on collision might seem very high, but the vehicles use a guidance system which is activated by wires buried in the concrete floor. As the service tunnel is considered to be part of a railway system, traffic follows the rule prevailing throughout Europe and drives on the left.

Two of the 5.6 mega-watt shuttle loco-motives were shipped to a test track in the Czech Republic, where they carried out an endurance test totalling some 50,000 km as well as brake perfor-mance tests at speed.

Before running the first trains through the Tunnel it was necessary to check that there was nothing protruding into their path. Test trains checked the loading gauge throughout the entire system.

On 20 June the first of the Transmanche Super Trains, now named Eurostar, was brought through the Tunnel from France to England. As the catenary was not yet energised it was towed through by a diesel locomotive.

July – December 1993

On 27 July Eurotunnel and TML announced a protocol under which control of the project would pass to Eurotunnel on 10 December. Thereafter TML would assist with the final tests required before the Intergovernmental Commission issued an Operating Certificate permitting the transport system to open to the public. The HGV

the Tests on Completion, the culmination of a long and complex commissioning process which had begun with the first equipment testing two and a half years previously.

The first systems to pass through this process had been the electrical substations, since the power they provided was needed for almost all the later tests. Work

Tourist shuttles would follow after the official opening of the Tunnel on 6 May by Her Majesty The Queen and President Mitterrand.

shuttle service would begin in the spring of 1994. Tourist shuttles would follow after the official opening of the Tunnel on 6 May by Her Majesty The Queen and President Mitterrand.

The project was now in its final phase. The tunnels were built, and practically all the systems were in place. Ahead lay the last acceptance tests before

on the other major subsystems began in the autumn of 1993: signalling, central control of the electrical and mechanical systems, radio, telephone, chilling plant, firemain, etc. A parallel series of tests had to be carried out with the rolling stock.

By 10 December, when the project was handed over to Eurotunnel, this commissioning programme was in progress.

At the controls of a
shuttle locomotive on
the French terminal.

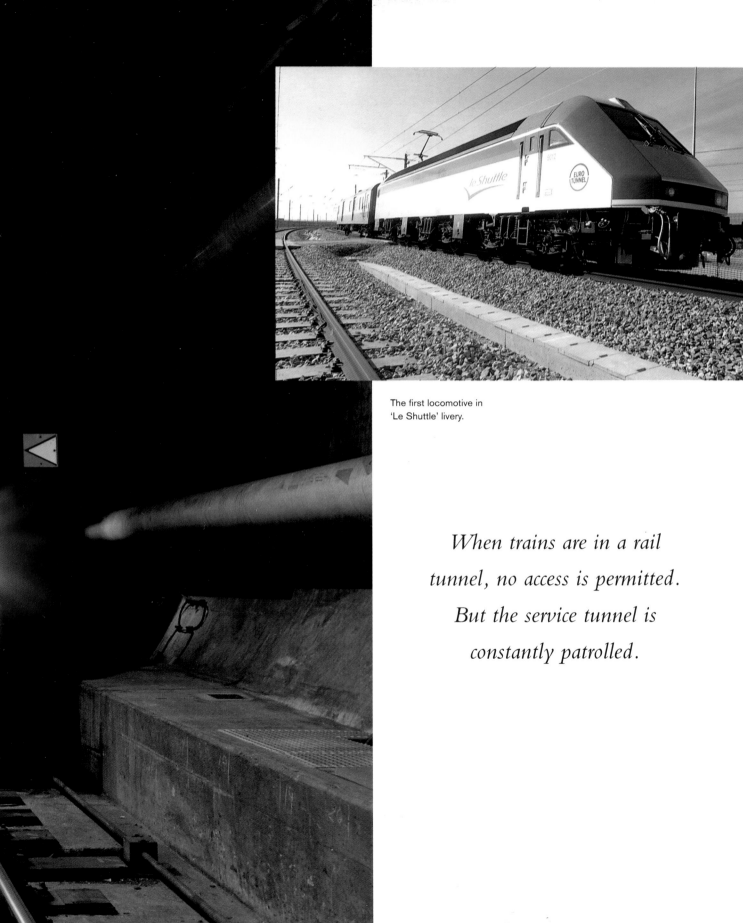

The first locomotive in
'Le Shuttle' livery.

*When trains are in a rail
tunnel, no access is permitted.
But the service tunnel is
constantly patrolled.*

A loading wagon for double-deck shuttles in the maintenance building with its lower-deck doors open. There are 18 of these loaders in the fleet.

View inside a double-deck shuttle with the fire-doors open. As on the Alpine car shuttles, the continuous internal roadway reduces boarding and exit times at the terminals. During the journey there are fireproof barriers with passenger pass-doors at the end of each wagon. The shuttle wagons are air conditioned and have an extremely powerful purging system to remove exhaust fumes.

One of the versatile 'Unimog' road/rail trucks shunting a double-deck shuttle wagon.

September: part of a tourist shuttle at the French terminal. A complete shuttle consists of 24 wagons, and is 800 m long.

The French portal.

The Sangatte site in
its final form.

The chiller plant at
Sangatte.

The Sangatte shaft
completed. The nor-
mal ventilation ducting
is on the right while
the huge SVS ducting
is on the left. A stair-
case has replaced the
construction-phase
passenger lifts.

The Sangatte site as it
appeared in August.
Contractors' buildings
were being demol-
ished and the final
landscaping was
under way.

*Sangatte and
Lower Shakespeare Cliff retain
a vital role in the system.*

The man standing on the right gives some idea of the size of the pipework below the dry-air cooler at Lower Shakespeare Cliff.

Lower Shakespeare Cliff in October.

The dry air cooler.

Landscaping at the western end of the Lower Shakespeare Cliff site.

Dusting pipes in the
service tunnel, which
is 50 km long.

Cleaning out cable trays.

The machine used to
clean the trackbed.

The tunnel construction, like most other
building work, left fine dust everywhere.
Before trains could pass through at speed,
the dust had to be removed by teams of
cleaners. Much could be achieved using
special equipment, but some jobs had to be
done by hand.

Washing the sides of
a rail tunnel.

During tests on the catenary in early November, a shuttle locomotive passed over the diamond crossing in the UK cross-over for the first time. Normally, the sliding cross-over doors would be firmly shut. Now that the lengthy process of commissioning had started, trains began to run through the tunnels with increasing frequency.

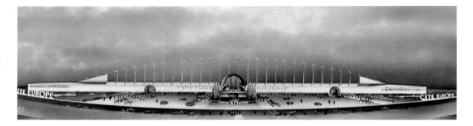

The first development on Eurotunnel's
100 hectare Cité de l'Europe site beside the toll
plaza is a huge shopping and leisure complex,
'Cité Europe', with hypermarket, boutiques and
a museum. The complex is open to the general
public as well as passengers using Le Shuttle.

The completed
control tower.

The Eurotunnel
Exhibition Centre.

Toll booths.

The French terminal:
elegant buildings and
open spaces.

The passenger terminal building, seen here nearing completion, is exclusively for those using Le Shuttle. It offers duty-free sales, a range of restaurants, shops, and other facilities.

The flyover leading into the terminal at the Fort Nieulay interchange.

A view over the French terminal in August. To the right of the toll plaza are car parks and the triangular passenger terminal building. The building site to the right of that is the future Cité Europe.

Aerial view of the platform area, showing the two overbridges for tourist vehicles boarding the shuttles, and *(right)* one of the exit bridges. In the foreground is the allocation area, where the length of the lanes corresponds exactly to space in the shuttle. To the right of the allocation area is the control tower, while the building in the foreground is the Exhibition Centre.

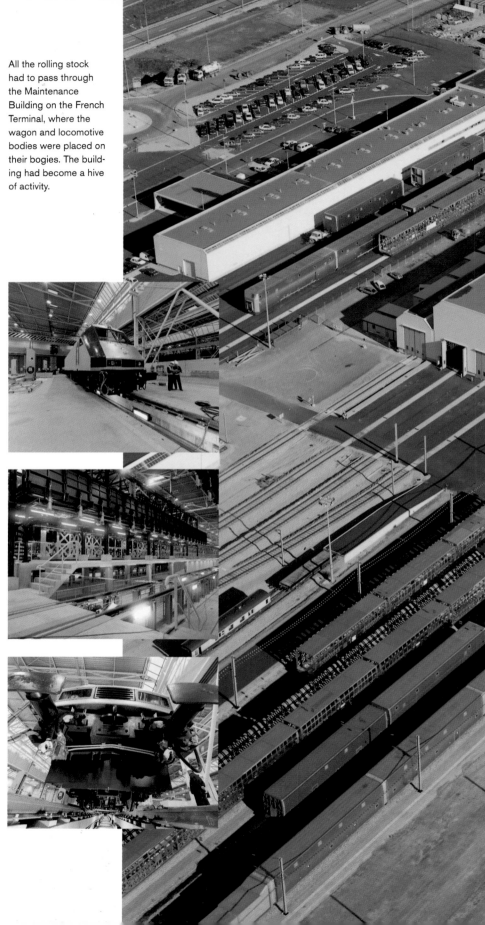

All the rolling stock had to pass through the Maintenance Building on the French Terminal, where the wagon and locomotive bodies were placed on their bogies. The building had become a hive of activity.

A shuttle locomotive in the Maintenance Building.

Raised platforms hinge down to give access to higher parts of the shuttle trains such as locomotive pantographs.

View under a shuttle locomotive.

A newly arrived shuttle
locomotive waiting for
its bogies.

*In the maintenance
building skilled
mechanics look after
the largest trains
in the world.*

The English terminal: a feat of planning.

The control tower.

The toll booths at dawn. The shuttle service will run 24 hours a day, 365 days a year.

The dominant features of the English terminal are still the Continental Main Line, the buried loop-tunnel and the platform area. Tolls, frontier controls, allocation, parking and the passenger services building are all concentrated on the lower left of this photograph. The HGV route is close to the boundary of the site. The most notable feature to the right of the Continental Main Line is the English maintenance building.

Finishing touches: polishing the floor inside the passenger terminal building.

The English maintenance building, far smaller than its French counterpart, is reserved for urgent or relatively minor tasks.

The passenger terminal building.

The Eurotunnel Exhibition Centre, which overlooks the terminal site from the southern side of the M20.

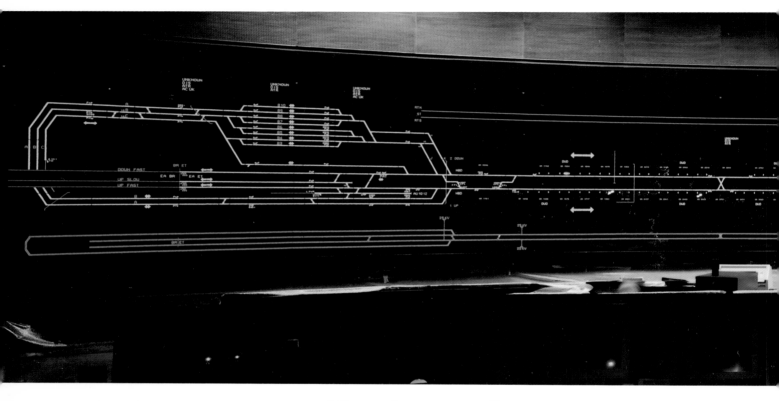

The railway controllers are among Eurotunnel's most highly trained staff. They must understand how every element in the system works.

The railway-system mimic panel in the Railway Control Centre is 24 m long and 3 m high. It uses digitised LED technology and is the largest of its kind anywhere. Under normal circumstances the railway system is controlled by computer, but controllers can intervene at various levels, if necessary right down to full manual control.

Roller shutters conceal the complex wiring behind the mimic panel which works in 'real time', reporting exactly what is happening in the system.

Inside the tunnels there are no train signals. Instead, the signalling system sends information through track circuits to a specially equipped console in front of the locomotive driver. Monitoring equipment tells the control system the exact position and speed of every train. If a driver were to ignore a signal to reduce speed, or failed to slow down sufficiently, an emergency braking system would automatically stop the train.

The journey through the system, whether for a car, coach or motorcycle, starts at the toll booth. Some drivers have prepaid tickets, others pay when they arrive. In either case there are no bookings for a particular departure time. Vehicles arriving at the terminal are put onto the first available shuttle.

Beyond the toll, on either side of the Channel, passengers have the choice of visiting the passenger terminal building or moving on towards the shuttle.

Using the Tunnel is not much more
complicated than driving along
a toll motorway.

Vehicles pass both British and French frontier controls before boarding the shuttle. There are no further controls on arrival.

From the allocation area where vehicles assemble for shuttle departures, it is only a short drive to the platform. It takes about 8 minutes to fill a shuttle.

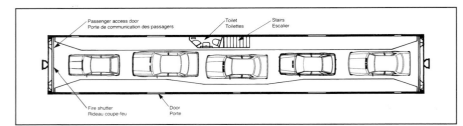

The shuttle is divided into two halves, each with a loading wagon at both ends. There are twelve single-deck wagons at the front of the train and twelve double-deck wagons at the rear. Double-deck shuttle wagons carry up to ten cars, while single-deck carriers can carry one coach, or three minibuses, or five cars. A shuttle loaded with 120 cars and twelve coaches is probably carrying about 800 passengers.

Shuttles have a locomotive at both ends. Either has sufficient power to haul the train on its own. The Chef de Train in the rear locomotive is a qualified driver. If it became necessary, in an emergency, the train could be divided in two and each half could leave the tunnel under its own power.

The journey from platform to platform is about 35 minutes, of which 26 are spent in the Tunnel.

The exit bridge leads straight to the motorway.
There is also access to local roads.

The speed and flexibil-
ity of the system takes
much of the stress out
of day-return visits.

British Rail, together with the French and Belgian state railways, have been important partners in the Eurotunnel project from a very early stage. Eurostar's frequent daily services between London and Paris (3 hours) and London and Brussels (3 hours and 10 minutes) will rival the best journey times available by air. There will be connections at Lille to other Continental cities. In 1996 further trains are to be introduced serving British cities beyond London, while overnight trains will link the capital with more distant centres on the Continent.

Eurostar services will rival air travel between London and Paris or Brussels.

Now that the British and Continental railway systems are directly linked, there is a huge potential for cross-Channel rail freight. This should be strongly competitive over long-haul European routes, and large investments have been made in the UK by Railfreight Distribution to provide regional terminals and the necessary rolling stock. Much of the traffic will consist of inter-modal containers which can be carried by road at each end of their journey. There will also be specialised traffic, such as trains delivering new cars and spare parts, as well as more traditional freight services.

*Freight vehicles follow
their own separate route
through the system.*

Like the tourist shuttles, HGV shuttles are divided into two sections. After boarding, drivers move their lorries forward along the shuttle 'roadway' until instructed to stop. They are then transferred, with any passengers, to the club car behind the leading locomotive.

As there are separate routes through the terminals for lorries, freight-vehicle services are unaffected by peak-season tourist traffic.

The time drivers spend away from their vehicles during the shuttle journey is sufficient to qualify for a statutory mid-shift break. Meals are served in the air-conditioned club car.

Electric points are available on the shuttle to power the refrigeration units of temperature-controlled vehicles, ensuring that the 'coolchain' is maintained throughout the journey.

Leaves fold down on each side of the HGV-loading wagon to provide a continuous roadway across two platforms. This gives drivers ample room to manoeuvre. During loading and unloading, when the weight of lorries is off-centre, the shuttle is rigidly supported by jacks.

At the English portal, the heads of the five UK partners of TML joined Sir Alastair Morton, Eurotunnel's Chief Executive, holding a symbolic chain which linked the flags of France and the United Kingdom. *(From left to right)*: Peter Costain (Costain), Tony Palmer (Taylor Woodrow), Neville Simms (Tarmac), Sir Alastair Morton, Joe Dwyer (Wimpey) and Sir Robert Davidson (Balfour Beatty).

On 10 December 1993, less than six and a half years after the ratification of the Treaty of Canterbury, TML handed the Channel Tunnel over to Eurotunnel. By then, work on the project had totalled some 170 million man hours.

Spectators *(from left to right)*: Frank Cain, previously Project Chief Executive of Eurotunnel, André Bénard, Sir Alastair Morton, Peter Costain, and Jean-Paul Parayre, the first French co-chairman of Eurotunnel and also a previous joint-chairman, with Peter Costain, of TML.

TML organised a spectacular ceremony in the platform area of the French terminal. After the English group had travelled through the tunnel, Sir Alastair Morton joined André Bénard in accepting the 'key' to the system.

Afterwards, the history of the project was told in a theatrical display of tableaux, moving shuttles and a son-et-lumière.

The scale of the tunnelling and terminal construction work is evident from the photographs in this book. It is far harder to grasp the extent and complexity of the equipment. Major systems are listed below.

MECHANICAL EQUIPMENT IN THE TUNNELS

- two ventilation systems (normal and supplementary) with their fan installations at Sangatte and Shakespeare Cliff.
- the cooling system, with its chiller and dry air cooler plants at Sangatte and Shakespeare Cliff.
- the drainage system with its pumping stations.
- the firemain system with its pumps and reservoirs.
- 600 special doors, including the doors of cross-passages and the two giant cross-over doors.

TRACK AND CATENARY

- 200 km of track, of which 100 km is in the tunnels.
- 176 sets of points, including the two diamond crossings in the cross-overs.
- the catenary system (950 km of cable and 15,000 supports).

ELECTRICAL DISTRIBUTION:

- two main substations connected to the British and French national grids, supplying 160 megawatts at 25,000 volts for locomotive traction (equivalent to a town of 250,000 inhabitants) and a three-phase 21,000 volt supply for other equipment.
- 175 secondary substations providing high, medium and low voltage supplies. There are 350 km of cable supports and more than 1,300 km of electrical supply cable in the tunnels.
- 20,000 lighting units, etc...

CONTROL AND COMMUNICATION

- a principal rail-traffic control centre on the English terminal, and a standby control centre on the French terminal, with their systems for controlling both rail traffic and the mechanical and electrical equipment. The entire system can be controlled from either centre.
- a traffic control centre on each terminal and associated monitors and road signals for controlling the movement of road vehicles.
- an in-cab signalling system in the tunnels, developed from the system used on the TGV Nord.
- a computerised real-time data transmission system handling 26,000 data sources, of which 15,000 are in the tunnels, linked by 238 km of fibre-optic cable.
- radio systems for communication and Eurotunnel's Concession Radio service, as well as a network of 1,200 telephones, public address, etc.

OTHER EQUIPMENT

- terminal services (drainage, reservoirs, pumps, water treatment, etc).
- service-tunnel transport vehicles and their equipment.
- miscellaneous equipment such as maintenance vehicles, etc.

SHUTTLES AND OTHER ROLLING STOCK

- 38 electric locomotives able to draw trains weighing some 2,400 tonnes at speeds up to 160 kph.
- 254 single-deck or double-deck tourist shuttle wagons.
- 272 wagons for HGV shuttles.
- 5 diesel locomotives with three exhaust scrubbers for operating in the tunnels.
- a fleet of specialised rolling stock for maintenance work in the rail tunnels.

QA Photos

'In the beginning, the engineers treated us with suspicion. After a while, when they saw that we were serious about our work and enthusiastic about theirs, they relaxed. In the end, they carried our bags, shared their sandwiches, told us their stories and kept us safe.'

Jim Byrne and Diana Craigie began covering Channel Tunnel news stories in 1985, as interest in the project revived. In January 1986 they were working on a press assignment in Lille when Eurotunnel were granted the concession to build and operate the Channel Tunnel.

This first contact with Eurotunnel led to a commission to cover the signing of the Channel Tunnel Treaty at Canterbury in February 1986. Soon afterwards they became Eurotunnel's official project photographers.

As the scale and diversity of the photographic work became apparent, Jim and Diana recruited staff and set up a separate company, QA Photos Ltd, to handle their work on the project in England and France. At first, QA Photos provided Eurotunnel with photographic and laboratory services, but the contract was soon enlarged to include the official Eurotunnel picture agency, the QA Photo Library, which distributes project photographs worldwide on Eurotunnel's behalf. Between 1986 and 1994 Jim and Diana, together with QA staff photographer Robby Whitfield, shot around 100,000 photographs. They 'got very muddy, had a lot of fun, and created a historic record of the Channel Tunnel project.' 501 of the 626 photographs in this book were taken for Eurotunnel by QA Photos.

Mike Griggs

Mike Griggs was trained as a photographer in the Royal Air Force photographic branch, a career which took him to South-East Asia, Northern Europe and North America. His responsibilities included the supervision of automated reconnaissance and of photogrammetric aircraft survey systems. He is now based in Dover, and joined TML as contract photographer shortly after the service-tunnel breakthrough in December 1990. Earlier, he had done some landscape photography for the Channel Tunnel Group before construction began.

This photograph of the first shuttle locomotive to cross the diamond crossing in the UK cross-over is an example of the challenge faced by photographers throughout the project. The catenary test programme allowed no time for photo opportunities. However, with co-operation from test engineers Martin Young and Alan Hevey a four-minute 'window' appeared, making it possible to capture this historic event. We gratefully acknowledge Mike's help. His photographs of the project are published by kind permission of Transmanche Link, and appear on: p.19 top, p.33 bottom left, p.71 centre right, p.96 left, p.97 top right, p.137 centre, lower left, p.154 (3), p.159 top left, p.165 bottom, p.168 bottom left, p.176 top right, p.187 (3), p.190 top right, p.198 top right, p.200 top right, p.202 top and bottom, p.203 (4), p.204 left and bottom, p.205 top right, p.206 bottom left, p.207 top and bottom left, p.208 bottom left, p.209, p.211 right, p.215 top left, p.216 bottom, p.217, p.220 left (3), p.221 top right, p.234 bottom right, p.236 bottom left.

Augusto da Silva

Augusto da Silva was born in Portugal in 1953 and moved to France when he was seven. Between 1979 and 1984 he worked mainly as a fashion photographer. He has also undertaken photographic reporting, notably in France, Portugal and north Africa.

In November 1988 Bouygues, one of the TML partner companies, commissioned him to photograph Channel Tunnel construction work on the French side. The experience of visiting the worksites impressed him deeply, and he came to an arrangement with TML which allowed him to return to the sites regularly. He was to spend days and nights photographing the giant tunnel boring machines and their crews, as well as many other aspects of the project. We gratefully acknowledge his help and his permission to reproduce the photographs appearing on: p.37 centre left, p.42 top right, p.53 top right, pp.65-6 bottom, p.105 (4), p.121 bottom right, p.193 right (2), p.228 right, p.237 bottom right.

Philippe Demail

After training as a photographer Philippe Demail worked for publishers and has undertaken numerous commissions to photograph towns such as Dublin, Berlin and Gdansk. He is deeply interested in architecture, especially as a subject for photography.

He has also made photographic reports on the activities of such places as the Paris airports and Carrefour hypermarkets. His photographs of famous people include government ministers.

Since the early days of the Channel Tunnel project he has made regular visits to the French tunnels and terminal by arrangement with Eurotunnel's Paris Press Office, and his photographs have appeared in Eurotunnel publications and "Eurotunnel News". He has tried throughout to capture the essence of the project, both in terms of physical construction and also 'men and women at work'.

We gratefully acknowledge his help and his permission to print the photographs on: p.22 top left, p.36 bottom (2). p.47 (all except top left), p.62 bottom left, p.80 top (2), p.136 centre left, p.206 top right, p.218 bottom left and right, p.219 top, p.232 top, p.233 bottom right, p.234 bottom left.

Phot'R

During his military service, Michel de Swarte served in the aerial photography section of the French army. He subsequently worked for ten years as an industrial photographer.

In 1964, while based at Valenciennes, he set up Phot'R. The company has specialised exclusively in aerial photographic work for industry. Phot'R moved to Lille Lesquin airport in 1970 and acquired a Cessna 172 aircraft fitted out for vertical and oblique photography.

In 1987 Eurotunnel awarded Phot'R a contract for aerial photography of the French sites. This has been particularly important since no other kind of photography could adequately portray a site as large as the terminal.

Photographs by Phot'R are: p.9 bottom, p.49 top right and bottom left, p.52 bottom, p.56 left, p.81 bottom, p.133 bottom, p.183 top, p.195 top, p.219 bottom right, pp.220-21 centre.

In addition we would like to thank the following for photographs or artwork:

Channel Tunnel Group Ltd.: p.18 top left, p.21 bottom, p.22 right.

P.-A. Decraene: p.28 bottom right, p.33 top right, bottom left, p.47 top left.

European Passenger Services: 'Eurostar' interior p.230 bottom left.

France-Manche S.A.: p.21 top, p.55 bottom right, p.218 top.

GEC-Alsthom: p.164 right, p.198 top left and bottom.

Russell Goddard: p.208 centre right.

Nathalie Jouan: p.136 centre right.

'La Vie du Rail', p.16 right.

Arthur Phillips for artwork on p.35 right.

J.-N. Pignet: p.167, third down.

Railfreight Distribution p.231 bottom.

V.D.Stokt: p.27 bottom right.

TML, for artwork: pp.10-11, pp.30-31 top, p.38 top, pp.102-3 top, p.123 top, p.142 top left, p.144 top, p.214 top left.

TML, for work by staff photographers on the French side: p.43 bottom (2), p.64 bottom, p.83 bottom left, p.97 bottom right, p.109 top left, bottom right, p.157 bottom left, p.158 centre left and right, p.166 top and centre left, p.186 top and bottom.

General acknowledgement

Finally, we would like to thank Martin Shirley and John Grover at Visible Edge, and also Anthony Mason and Keith Law for their assistance. No thanks would be sufficient for all those in Eurotunnel and TML - too many to name - who have helped us so willingly with this book. We gratefully acknowledge 'The Link' and other publications by TML and Eurotunnel which we have plundered for facts. Every effort has been made to check the information and to seek clarification where sources conflicted. If, despite this, there are errors, they are ours alone.

Further reading

The Eurotunnel Exhibition Centre, St Martin's Plain, Folkestone, Kent CT19 4QD issues and stocks a wide range of educational, general and technical publications about the Channel Tunnel, including a useful series of bibliographies. These publications are available to visitors or by mail order.